Blackberries and Golden Wattle

Hilda Metcalf Hunt

Blackberries and Golden Wattle

The Thorns and Beauty of a Childhood in the Adelaide Hills

Blackberries and Golden Wattle: The Thorns and Beauty of a Childhood in the Adelaide Hills
ISBN 978 1 76041 966 0
Copyright © Jean McArthur 2020

First published 2020 by
GINNINDERRA PRESS
PO Box 3461 Port Adelaide 5015
www.ginninderrapress.com.au

Contents

Introduction	7
Metcalf Family Tree	9
Hunt Family Tree	10
Bishop Family Tree	11
Beginnings	13
Florence Marian Bishop (21 February 1874–8 May 1972)	15
The Bishops	18
Granny Hunt	20
Dad	22
The 1914–18 War	24
Ethel Appledore	25
Tuberculosis	28
Gordon	29
Schooldays I	31
Schooldays II	34
Train Kids	37
Bread	38
School Lunches	39
By Steam Train	40
The Forgotten Jacket	43
The Institute Hall	44
Circus	46
Oakbank	47
Itinerant Travellers	48
Grimes	50
Auntie Maud	51

Bill Paech	54
The New Chediston	55
Tommy Hunt	59
Odds and Ends	62
Market Day	64
No Seamstress	66
Show Days	68
Old Jack Ross	69
Galahs	70
Curlew	71
Here and There on Western Flat	72
Friends and Neighbours	74
Hillford Farm	76
When We Were Younger	79
Macclesfield Road	83
Poisoned Hand	84
Water	85
Washing Day	88
A Glimpse of Beauty	91
Tannery	92
Autumn	95
Lights	96
Wood	97
Easter Time	98
Dunny Cart	100
Comparisons	102
Horses	104
Echunga Road	107
Hammond	109
High School – 1929 and 1930	113
Barmera	115
Blakiston	117
Postscript	118

Introduction

This is a collection of memories from our mother, Hilda Metcalf McArthur, née Hunt, between the years of 1912 to 1936. Although not unique, they justify recording as her childhood was very different from those of today's children. She wrote these episodes over a period of ten years. We are proud to have collated them.

Jean L. McArthur

Christina F. Carr

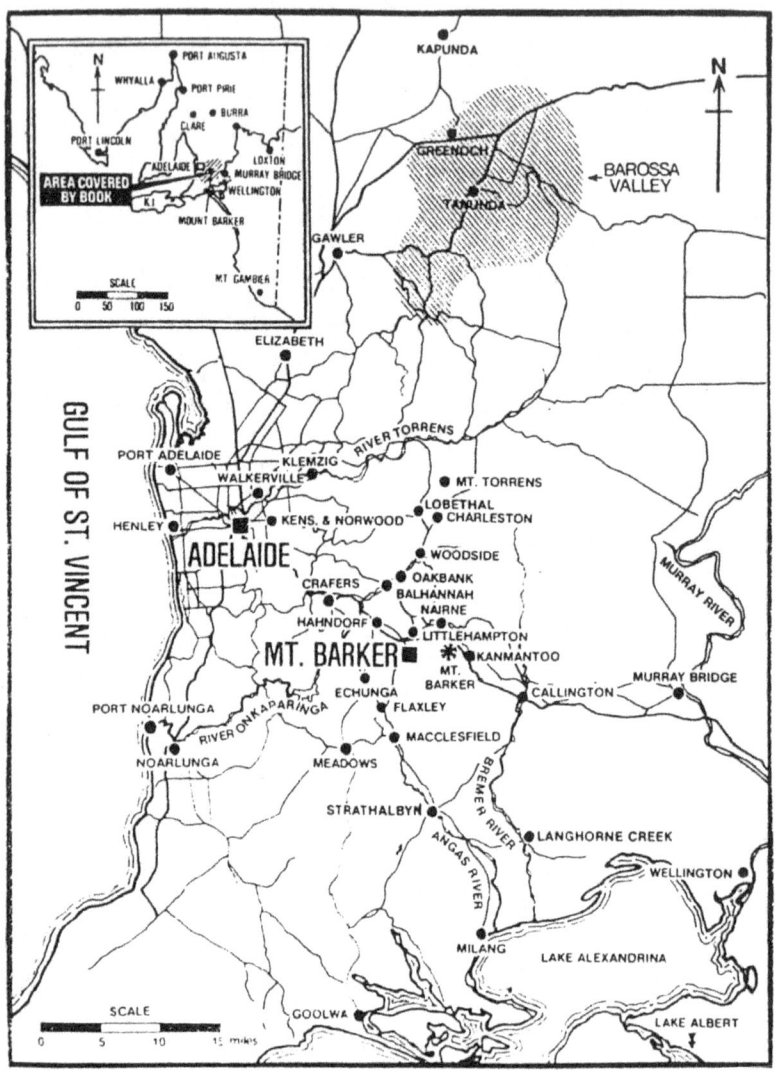

Metcalf Family Tree

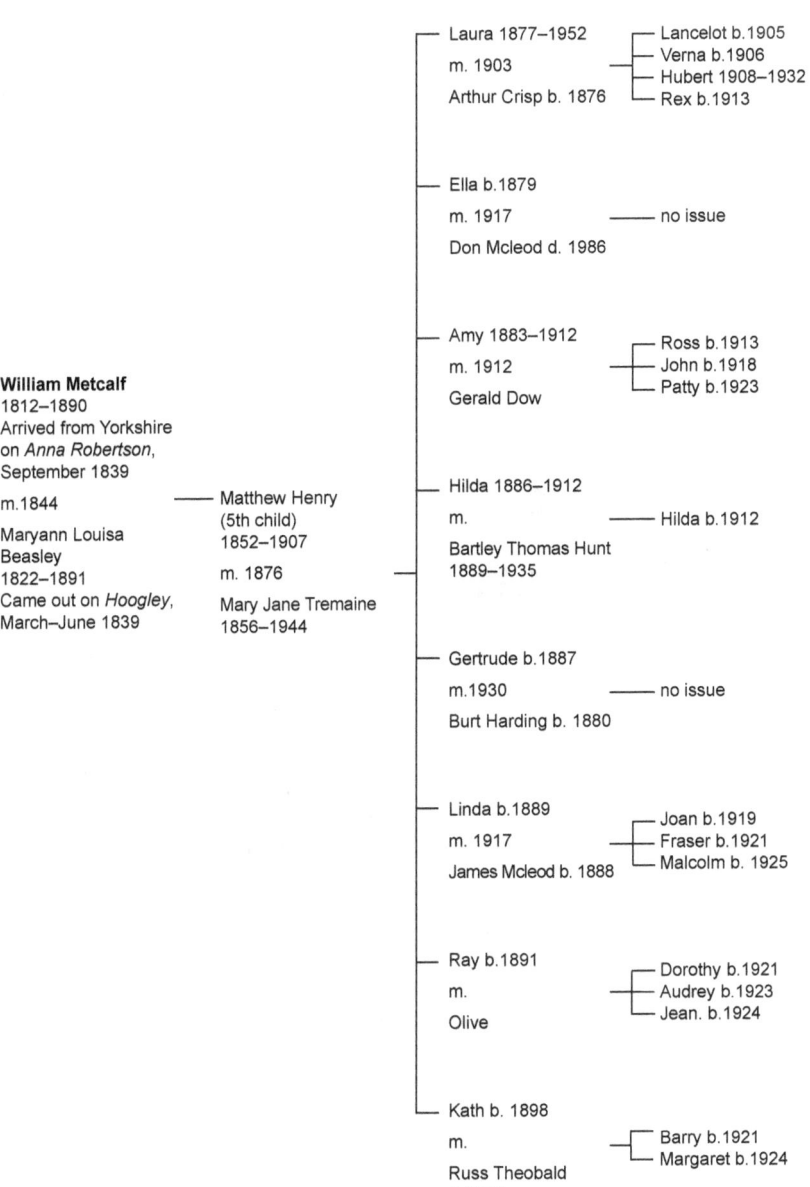

Hunt Family Tree

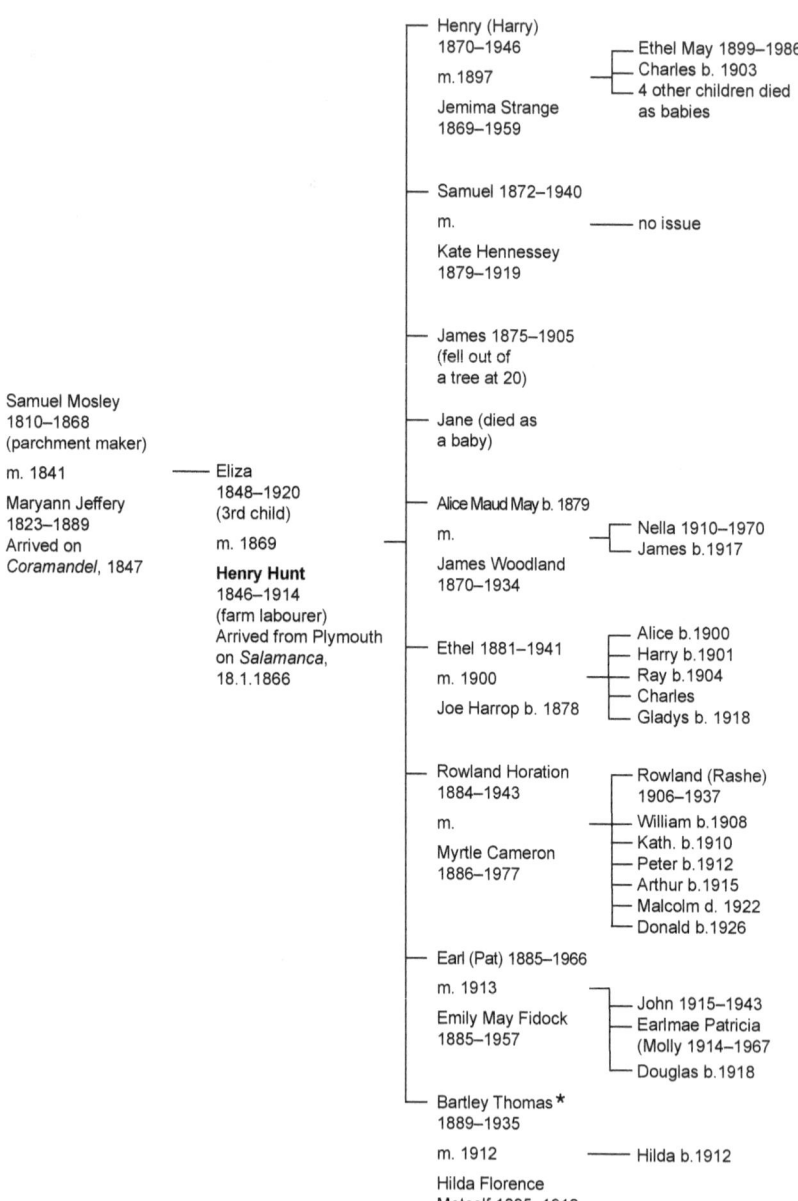

* Since our mother wrote this, it has been found that Bartley Thomas Hunt's name was probably Bartlett.

Bishop Family Tree

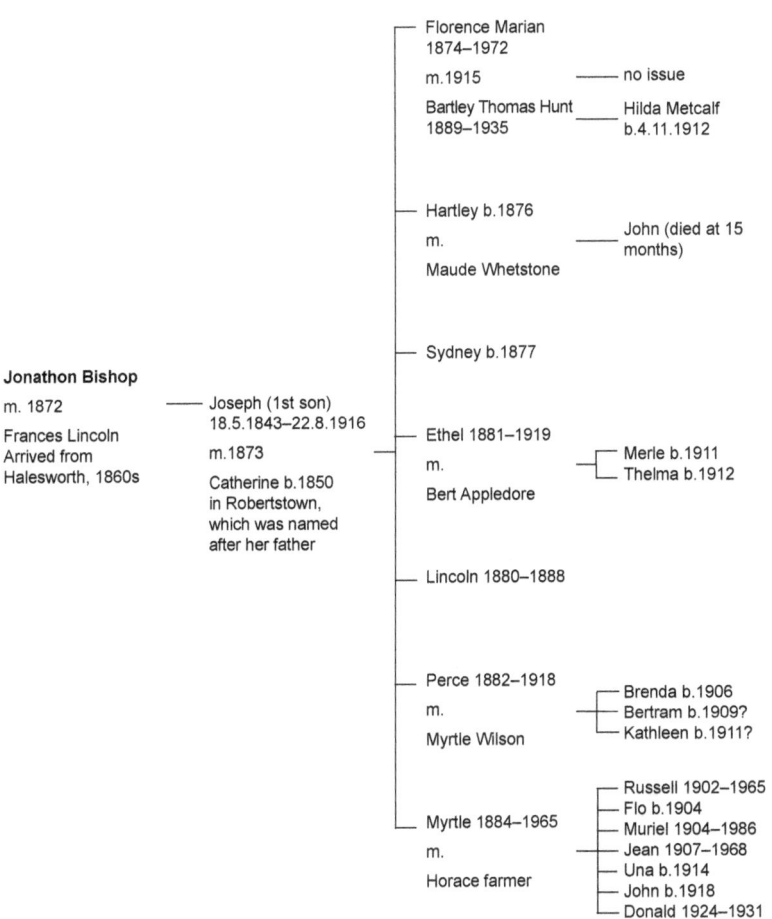

For my grandchildren

Beginnings

If I have a totem, it must surely be the grey thrush, for he sang outside the window of a little house at Bugle Ranges on the day of my birth, which sadly, was the day of my mother's death. My father told me that the last thing my mother spoke of was that thrush's song.

My father was the youngest of the Hunt family. I was cared for by Aunt 'Mime', wife of Harry Hunt, the eldest brother, until I was three years old. I can still see Aunt Mime, a small hard-working lady, out milking cows or in the little lean-to kitchen surrounded by the aroma of fresh baking. Memories of that time are few but clear. Dad often came to see me on his way from Granny Hunt's to his work in Davidson's orchard. I would follow him from Auntie Mime's along the track, just as far as the slip rails, then he would send me back to the house, where the purple hardenbergia grew.

Uncle Harry, who always seemed to be busy outside, was the only man I knew with a beard. He caught hares which the local hotel proprietors bought. The hares were gutted but not skinned, well dressed with pepper and hung on the back veranda until the next trip to town. Presumably the pepper was sufficient to keep the blowflies at bay!

Mime and Harry's daughter May was fourteen years older than I, her brother Charlie was about nine. Charlie had a pet magpie which was the bane of my life. He delighted in chasing me everywhere, pecking at my ankles. When I ran away and jumped down a cutting (made for a cellar which never eventuated), Maggie jumped on my head!

My cousin May took me to visit our grandparents, Eliza and Henry Hunt, one day. It was across paddocks along a track which I later often took alone, past the waterhole with the huge blackwood tree growing on its bank. We saw a roan cow and calf grazing in the house paddock. My only memory of my grandfather is of a bearded man sitting near a sunny window in a rocking chair with a rug over his knees. In later times, I slept in that same room. At the time of his death, I was twenty-months old, so children do remember from an early age.

Florence Marian Bishop
(21 February 1874–8 May 1972)

In front of Bennett and Fisher's office in Mt Barker's Gawler Street, my Aunt Mime and others were talking to a woman who was a stranger to me. She was better dressed than they and spoke with self-assurance.

I stared at her because she was different. Later, she became my stepmother. My father married Florence Marian Bishop in July 1915.

Often, she told me that she thought I was peculiar because of the way I had looked at her on our first meeting; indeed, she almost succeeded in convincing me many times over.

Of course, times were hard, money scarce and life as a struggling farmer's wife was a long downward step from her former positions. A family help was considered an honourable occupation in the Victorian era. She had even been companion to people named Le Messurier who travelled to England for Queen Victoria's Jubilee celebrations in 1898. They spent six months in Italy before returning.

Looking back, I fancy her outstanding quality was her compassion and support for others who were ill or in need. Unfortunately, her sudden fierce temper and acid tongue lost her many friends.

Marian was the eldest child of Joseph and Catherine Bishop, who owned a shop in Port Lincoln and also managed the post office. She remembered her childhood as a happy time, although it must have been busy, as six other children were born and one small boy died.

When a small girl, she had a walking, talking doll which said 'Mumma' and 'Pappa', a real novelty in the 1870s.

She remembered the weekly bath on Saturdays after which the children were given an apple each and allowed to eat it walking along the beach in their clean clothes. Sometimes, they gathered cranberries (possibly muntries) in the hummocks.

Once, she took her young brothers out into the bay in a flat-bottomed boat. Her mother was naturally very upset at the risk Marian was taking. She stood on the beach waving frantically until they returned.

About 1880, her mother developed cataracts in her eyes. The local doctor suggested that she go to Mt Gambier for treatment, as a suitably qualified doctor was there. For this purpose, she boarded Captain Underwood's vessel, which regularly ran from Port Lincoln to Hobart, stopping off at south-eastern ports en route.

When Marian was twelve years old, her mother died suddenly, from a haemorrhage after a miscarriage. She went to live with her Bishop grandparents and the other children lived with various members of her father's family. Baby Myrtle became a ward of the state and was fostered by Mrs Cook at Minlaton, York Peninsula. That appeared to have been a happy arrangement.

In 1890, Joseph Bishop married a widow with two school-aged children. They gathered Marian and the other children and travelled on the first train from Burra to Broken Hill. Mr Bishop was the first postmaster at Broken Hill. It proved not to be a very satisfactory time for them. Mr Bishop was walking past the local pawnshop and happened to see his silver watch in the window! There were other incidents such as official cheques being embezzled. It seemed that the new Mrs Bishop was not honest and he was forced to leave the post office. The marriage was dissolved.

The elder boys found work in Broken Hill. I'm not sure about the other children at that time. The father joined a religious group and eventually went to Zion City near Chicago in the United States of America, taking his son by his second marriage with him.

Marian ran away to her grandparents, where she lived until after their deaths. Later, she worked as a companion with various families. She would easily take offence from her employers and leave, going to her sister Myrtle's place until she obtained a new position. Cousin Flo remembers the cab pulling up unexpectedly at their front gate, her mother pulling back the curtain and whispering, 'It's Marian again!'

When she accompanied Mrs Le Messurier to England for Queen Victoria's Golden Jubilee, she was able to meet some of her English relatives. The expression in my youth was that visiting England was 'going home', even if you and your parents had been born in Australia.

It was when she was employed as a companion-help at Edgar Davidson's 'Baruna' property at Mt Barker that she met my father. The Davidsons were well-to-do people who had planted a large apple orchard. When I was a schoolgirl, they exported apples labelled with crossed swords to England. They also had a Romney sheep stud.

My father had been employed by Mr Davidson to install pipes to drain waterlogged land from part of the orchard.

No doubt married life, once her sister Ethel* had passed away, with hard work and little money, was very disheartening. Dad also drank too much wine sometimes. She did leave once and was absent about a week. It seems her brother Hartley persuaded her to return.

---

* Ethel Appeldore – see page 25.

The Bishops

Marian's Grandfather Bishop had been a 'gentleman farmer' in England. He came to South Australia with his family bringing a Manning cottage* to erect on the property known as 'Bishop's Court' near Milang.

Poor fellow had no idea of farming in a new and raw country. It proved a disaster, for the property had to be sold and the family scattered. Even household contents were sold, including a solid silver cutlery service, Mother told me.

Mr Bishop was a very gentle person much loved by his family. He was admired by his grandchildren and the great-grandchildren still repeat stories about him.

He was deaf. One stormy day he met a crony in the street. During the conversation, he was asked, 'And how is Mrs Bishop?'

* Manning cottage (extract from *Adelaide Advertiser*, Friday 17 February 1989) Recently a discussion began on Manning cottages. We know they were designed and made in England and shipped to South Australia in the holds of ships as residences for some of our early settlers. I know of three of these. I presume they were of timber construction but would be glad if you could give me more details; for example, what type of roofing was used. Were they an early version of modular construction, or of limited design and size? H.M.M. (Beachport).
Manning cottages were originally erected with a sailcloth or canvas roof, and later the specification was amended to boarded roofs with tarred felt covering. Their design was of a modular, add-on type, and based on timber floorplates and top-plates, separated by vertical posts which slotted into these pieces. The spaces between these posts could be filled with Baltic pine wall panels, window panels or door panels, depending on the differing needs of the individual site. The roof was not a load-bearing part of the structure, and usually rested on the top plate, sometimes being roped to the box section. The houses were designed by English architect Henry Manning of High Holborn, London, and were built in Britain for export to the colonies. Examples were exported to Africa, Jamaica, Sierra Leone, New Zealand and the eastern States of Australia.

Thinking that his friend was speaking of the weather, Grandfather replied, 'Very windy, very windy'!

Mrs Bishop after so many hardships became a very careful person, living frugally. Fish heads bought at the city market were an economcal buy for meals.

The old couple lived in a little house in Leader Street, Goodwood. Marian lived with them at times and cared for her grandfather until his death in his ninety-second year. His wife predeceased him by a couple of years.

Granny Hunt

Like most country women of the late 1880s and the early twentieth century, she would have been a busy, hard-working woman.

Born Eliza Moseley in 1847, she married Henry Hunt on 11 January 1869. They had nine children; only three were girls, one of whom died as a baby.

Henry Hunt was born in 1846 and became a stonemason and general builder. There were no unions to decide who should build the walls, do the carpentry or put on the roof. Grandfather could do it all and taught his sons to do the same.

He was often absent from home all week, returning only on Saturday afternoon and leaving again on Sunday with fresh food supplies for the next week. At one time he built additions to the hotel at Wellington. He also built 'Mindacowie' at Middleton and when the Peterborough to Broken Hill railway line was put through, he worked on the construction of railway cottages at stations along the line, which was opened in 1890.

He and Granny lived at the foot of Windmill Hill with their family and the last time I passed that way some pear trees were still growing there. Later, the family moved to what was known as Western Flat, where Dad was living with Granny after my mother died.

When he remarried, he took his new bride to live there. I was about three years old when I left Auntie Mime's to live with my new stepmother.

As I remember her, Granny seemed to be an old lady wearing a dark frock – traditionally elderly women wore black. She would be sitting in a rocking chair in one of the front rooms of the house and welcomed my visits.

On one such occasion, Mother accused her of giving me a sip of wine. I do not remember her doing so, but I do remember the unholy row which followed. It ended when Granny and her possessions were packed off to a little cottage in the lane behind Bell's store in Mt Barker. One theory was that Mother was pregnant at the time of Granny Hunt's eviction. It was presumed that there was a miscarriage.

I often visited Granny with my dad and when I attended school I would slip in to see her during the lunch hour until her sudden death in 1920.

Mother could not abide her and seemed to think that I was like her in some ways. She taunted me about my high forehead and, when I acquired styes on my eyelids, about the lashes falling out 'just like your ugly old grandmother's'.

Mother made some pretty frocks for me but I dreaded trying them on for I never failed to get a sharp forefinger poked into my stomach with a caustic remark.

'Hold your stomach in. It sticks out like your Grandmother's.'

Poor old Granny. I never thought of her as ugly. To me, she was just my Granny. Of course, I realised that she was older than anyone else I knew, but she was always kind to me and I felt comfortable with her.

Dad

How I loved going with my dad when he was working in the paddocks, cutting wood for fenceposts or firewood or just clearing up a tree which had been blown over. He might have wattles to strip of their bark. I could help strip wattle bark too.

He would show me a robin's nest or where the blackbird built on an old stump, the regrowth hiding it from general view.

He taught me to plait using the stems of the clumpy rush-like growths we called tussocks which were forty to fifty centimetres high and grew plentifully on uncleared land. Making bangles for my arm was easier or even a ring for a finger. One pulled out a single strand, made a circle large enough to go over my hand, and twisted the other end of the rush until it was nearly used up before adding and twisting a second, third or even fourth, depending on the thickness I wanted.

There were wild flowers and lizards and ants which ran up my legs if I stood on their nests. That was when I learnt that if I should do something wrong, what Dad told me would happen, usually did. The word 'don't' didn't seem to come in to his vocabulary. He told me that if I stood too near a meat ants' hill, the ants would run up my legs. Well, ants working on their nests are very interesting to watch and of course I gradually got too close. Wow! Did those ants nip! But naturally Dad came to my rescue and brushed me down. Jumping ants had a fierce sting; inch ants seemed lonely black or reddish chaps wandering along and fascinating to just watch.

I find it difficult to tell about my father, with whom I had a kind of tacit understanding. I learnt early in life that Dad could not talk to me about my own mother for fear of upsetting Mother. What disquiet and unnecessary trauma jealousy can cause. I only once remember Dad speaking of the one happy year he spent with my mother. Mother Marian heard of this and promptly accused Dad of 'trying to turn the child against me'. At that time, I may have been six-years old.

Poor woman, her sudden bursts of violent temper were her downfall and the people to whom 'I will never speak again' were numerous and possibly were not worried by her silence to them! She could be thoughtful and helpful but one always had to step gently towards her.

One night soon after he had remarried, Dad disapproved of Mother's treatment of me so he picked me up out of my bed and carried me back to Auntie Mime's, carefully wrapping my feet in a blanket to keep them warm.

Dad was really such a gentle man and, as Auntie Myrt Farmer said, helpful and understanding. Yes, he occasionally came home from Mt Barker partially intoxicated, which naturally was a worry to us all, but only once did I ever know him to really lose his temper and lay down the law. We were cutting melon for jam at the time and one chopping board was permanently indented where he rammed the but of his pocketknife down to emphasise his annoyance!

The 1914–18 War

Cousin May's fiancé Charlie Jensen was a Dane. The only time I remember seeing a soldier in full uniform was when he came to say goodbye to us. He joined the Australian Imperial Forces and marched away, never to return. May was very pleased to receive a portmanteau containing some of his belongings after the war. She used the portmanteau as a sort of shopping bag for years.

In 1919, May married Harry Fidock, the youngest brother of Emily Hunt, wife of our Uncle Pat. This made May Uncle Pat's sister-in-law as well as his niece! Uncle Pat's correct name was Earl Alexander.

*

Some years previously, typhoid fever had left Dad with an impairment of the heart. He did not therefore pass his medical test and was not acceptable to the army. To his humiliation and disgust, he was once handed a white feather, a symbol of cowardice.

*

When there was an election, old Zilm really hit high and hard. His ballot paper was of a different colour from that of the Popes, Hunts, Camerons or Stevensons, because his name was of German origin.

'I have lived here all my life. I have a son somewhere over there in France and you insult me like this!'

I bet he added a few '*Gott en Himmels*' and other words besides.

Old Zilm drove a small trolley (a platform with turnable front wheels) drawn by two well kept grey horses.

Ethel Appledore

Mother's sister Ethel Appledore had two daughters, Merle and Thelma, the latter about my age. When Ethel's husband Bert went overseas with the army, the family came to live with 'old maid' Miss Daniels, in a little brick cottage in Mt Barker.

One day in the small lean-to kitchen where it was warm by the wood stove, she dropped her knitting needle. On bending to pick it up, she found that it had disappeared down a crack in the floor into a well almost full of water! It would seem that it had been the original water supply for the house prior to building the lean-to. Aunt Ethel was not exactly happy to know that she was frequently walking over a well of water, even though it did appear to have been securely covered!

Auntie Ethel had tuberculosis and when her condition worsened, she came to live with us until her death in October 1919. She was a thin woman with friendly blue eyes and fair straight hair, which she often wore in plaits. At first she used a small lean-to room in the back veranda but was later moved into the front bedroom where Granny Hunt had stayed.

She constantly knitted socks: for soldiers, for her daughters and sometimes for me. I particularly remember a black pair with shiny red thread spun through the wool.

Aunt Ethel was most patient with me. She taught me basic sewing stitches, how to knit and tie knots in cotton. We used knitting cotton and stiff steel needles with corks from eau de cologne bottles on the ends to prevent the stitches slipping off. The cologne was used as a rub for the skin over her pressure points, so corks were in plentiful supply.

I would go needle through the loop, thread over and around, needle

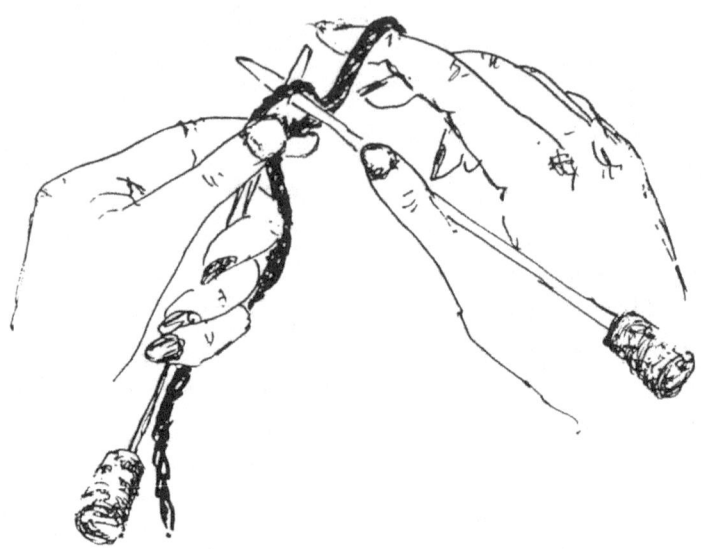

out and thread off; another stitch made. There were dropped stitches often, but she always quietly picked them up again.

She was a good storyteller. From her, I also learned my alphabet and began to read. On the wall were printed texts which she read to me.

> Through the long night watches,
> May thine angels spread,
> Their white wings above me,
> Watching round my bed.

Visitors often came; relatives, the Salvos or Dr Wunderley called regularly. Mrs Grimes noticed if someone came while Mother was out and would make up afternoon tea to bring over. She trudged down her hill, across the road and up our steeper rise with a laden tray.

When Ethel became really ill, her youngest sister Auntie Myrt Farmer came to stay, bringing with her one of her twin daughters, Flo. My father had cut up some dry sheoak logs for roaring fires which burnt all night in the living room. One of the sisters or Dad would alternately sit up to watch the very sick woman.

In her bottom drawer, she had a special nightdress for her final garment. When laid out, her hands were crossed on her breast with small flowers between her fingers. Everyone went in to view her before her body was placed in the coffin.

I have always felt that this experience of death in the home was a good one for me, as there was a comforting sense of understanding between us all.

Sometimes, I thought that Marian married my father to have a home where she could care for her sick sister.

Bert Appledore's sister took the two girls to live with her until their father came home from the front. He later remarried and they lived on the land in Eastern Victoria.

Tuberculosis

During the early 1900s, tuberculosis (known as consumption or TB), was a common disease especially among the poorer communities where crowded living conditions were common. Damp houses and poor nutrition added to the problem. As it was contagious, sometimes entire families were affected.

One form, referred to as 'galloping consumption', where the patient became violently ill with high temperatures, sudden loss of weight and general debility, would take its victim in three to four months.

More commonly, TB was insidious, a much less dramatic condition. The patient had a persistent cough, usually for some years, eventually causing lung haemorrhages before death. In the late 1920s and the 1930s, there was much study of the causes and new treatments were developed until now it has been almost completely eradicated.

Gordon

It was decided, I think, that I should be better off with a companion when walking to school and to share life. Well, early in 1920 before the school term began, this strange but neat eight-year-old city boy arrived from Bowden, an Adelaide suburb.

His name was Gordon Dunstall. He was the second of six children. I remember only that his older brother's name was Harry and nothing about his family. How strange it must have been for him coming to live on a farm where we milked cows and reared fowls, ducks and turkeys.

Neighbours were not close, although we could see one house, and Uncle Pat lived at the top of the gulley past the large blackwood tree and waterhole where the stock came to drink. It was at this spot I remember laughing heartily at the new chum who found himself standing on a poor sleepy lizard when Dad and I were taking Gordon to introduce our place to him.

Whether or not Gordon was good for me I could not say, but we wandered to and from school for six years. We picked peas from Ben Paech's crop beside the road and enjoyed eating them. Later on, Gordon managed to acquire apples from the neglected orchard behind the briar hedge near the butcher's slaughter house. Unfortunately, he also took a liking to other children's lunches. Exactly why I do not know as our own lunch should have been sufficient. We had two full rounds of bread, one with meat and sauce, the other with jam and butter, plus cake or pastry and some fruit. There was always something to eat and drink when we arrived home each afternoon. The lunch pinching caused quite a deal of consternation at school and among our family.

We had two or three goats, one being a billy with longish upright horns. Dad bought a beautiful leather harness for the goat and made a cart. What fun we had harnessing Billy into the cart. He could pull it quite well too.

One day, we took Billy and cart onto the road and were some distance from home when a smartly stepping horse in a neat buggy was driven down the hill towards us. The horse, it seemed, had never seen such a spectacle. He pranced and stood up on his hind legs, tilting the cart to a precarious angle. His owner was somewhat irate and ordered us and our contraption to the side of the road well out of his and his animal's sight.

We made our way home but were never again allowed to take Billy out on the road. The harness hung in the shed for many years but was seldom used and eventually disappeared, as did various other things. No doubt Gordon would have known what happened to them. Mother suspected that he sold them.

Gordon was a very good liar, a fact which sometimes got us both out of hot water. It did on the afternoon he came into my room after school while I was changing my clothes. I asked him to go out. He refused and came closer. I picked up my boot and hit him on the head with the heel, which was well shielded by a metal protector. His head certainly bled but we had it cleaned up before the parents arrived home. Gordon glibly told Mother he had fallen out of a gum tree and hit his head on a rock. Of course I agreed that it was a nasty gash!

We had splendid times together and also squabbled as most children would. We grew up and Gordon left school, working for various neighbours. I think that his lunch-stealing episodes and lying made people wary of his honesty. Suddenly he left home and I never saw him again. I believe he called on the Farmer family after leaving Mt Barker and once, many years later, Flo saw him.

Schooldays 1

It was in 1920 when I joined a group of twenty or more six- and seven-year-olds on our first day at Mt Barker Primary School. Most of us were driven there in a horse-drawn trap or buggy (a two-or four-wheel carriage with a fold-down hood) that morning, but from then on, we walked four or more kilometres each way and were expected to be home again by five p.m.

Aunt Ethel, who died three months earlier, had taught me many elementary tasks, including arithmetic, writing and reading. However, I found the sounding method of 'c-a-t cat'; and 'd-o-g dog' in our grade I primers a big help. With the use also of 'look and say' words like 'the', 'do' and 'there', reading became a delight. The grade II primers gave us examples of double vowel sounds like 'ea' in peach, 'a-e' in take; and 'oo' in book and so on. These two primers were in use in schools for many years.

My desk mate was Reta Pope and we shared our double desks for most of the next seven years. The desks had a ledge underneath for books. There was a groove along the top for chalks and later pencils and pens. Two wire frames were placed upright on the front edge to place our blackboards, which were about twelve inches (thirty centimetres) square. We used mainly white chalk for writing. The three-ply wooden boards were cleaned each Friday afternoon in the long hand-washing trough in the boys' shelter shed. I think that these boards were then painted with ink. In the upper school grades, the inkwells were collected emptied and washed ready for refilling next Monday morning.

Early reading books seemed to have been of British origin, for they never told us anything about Australia or had Australian stories. *Tom and the Water Babies* was one of the first books I read without help.

Some things puzzled me. For instance, I had no idea what sea anemones into which Tom popped pebbles were like. I knew only of the bright red anemone flowers which Mother grew in her garden. Another puzzle was that Tom went to a place called 'nowhere' – now here. Some time later, I found the word was actually 'no-where'!

From Grade III onwards, the monthly arrival of *Children's Hour* (a small, popular monthly booklet for primary school children) was always welcome! These contained mainly Australian stories, poems, stories from other places, and some black and white illustrations.

Miss Gwen Cook taught grades I and II in a large classroom. On the end wall, a bell rope dangled and, on a signal from the teacher, one of the boys would ring the bell to tell the whole school of lesson time changes, recess and lunch hours. There were three lessons before morning recess then two before lunch, two before afternoon recess and two afterwards.

There were four terms per year until 1923, when a three-term year was introduced. There was also a sudden influx of children in the lower grades that year, resulting from the return of ex-servicemen from World War I. So a partition was placed in our large classroom, grades I and II separated and another teacher employed.

Grades III and IV gathered in the next room where Miss Jean Pearce carefully wrote the date on the right-hand corner of the wall-length blackboard. She especially pointed out to us the twenty-second of February 1922 as a significant date – 22-2-22!

It was in these two classes that we began chanting our arithmetic tables, all printed neatly on both ends of the board until we could answer Miss Pearce's multiplication or division questions without hesitation. Other lessons were reading, history, dictation and transcription. Each Friday morning, a weekly test was held and it was our aim to obtain four sums correct and no errors in dictation or spelling. Weekly tests continued for the rest of primary school.

Every Wednesday afternoon, all classes had sewing lessons for girls and woodwork for the boys. We learned to 'tack', 'run', 'hem', 'run and fell' and so on on small calico samples with pink or blue cotton. The samples were then stitched into an exercise book. Other handiwork included stitches on simple doilies. These were not my favourites, for my stitches were uneven and satin stitch was never smooth like most of the other girls' work.

It was also in grade III that we learned to write with pen and ink. Reta, my desk mate, made neat round letters, well shaped with no blots. I found holding the pen correctly very difficult. New nibs issued every Monday soon would be 'crossed' as I scratched and blotted my way across the pages. I sometimes felt that the harder I tried, the more disreputable my writing became. My fingers were always ink-stained. The one consolation was that Alice, the lass who sat in front of us, was no better than I.

Spelling books for the upper grades contained rules such as 'i before e except after c'; words with similar spelling but different sounds like 'cough', 'rough' and 'through'; words of similar sounds but different meanings – 'sent', 'scent' and 'cent'. Examples were listed on each page or put into sentences. One I remember was 'Tell Hugh to hew down the yew tree.'

'Trace' was a word which confused me. We used tracing paper and traced maps and designs. Horses were attached to a gig or buggy with strong stitched leather traces. With large vehicles, chains were used and called trace chains. Mother after working or walking in the paddocks would report having seen traces of rabbits. Eventually, I realised that 'nice' people never spoke of having seen a rabbits' dung heap, or even cow dung; that was cow manure or droppings!

History was chiefly of English kings, battles, events and dates, such as Battle of Hastings 1066. Australian history seemed to refer more to Captain Cook's discoveries, early convict settlement, or Flinders and his exceedingly accurate maps of our coastline. One must not forget the early inland explorers: Burke and Wills, Sturt, Edward John Eyre and so on. Of course we were told of attacks by natives but no one ever mentioned until very recent years how abominably some of the early settlers treated the 'blacks'.

Schooldays II

About two hundred and forty children attended the Mt Barker Primary School. There was also a small Catholic primary school, as well as a girls' convent for boarders and day pupils.

In the early schooldays, we played at hide and seek and skipping, but later came rounders and basketball (netball) for girls or cricket and football for the boys. Marbles were another favourite with the boys. I was never very good at any of the ball games.

At nine-twenty, the sound of the third bell called all pupils of the school to assemble. The lower grades grouped in the smaller portion of the yard, whilst the higher grades were nearer their classrooms. The drum and fife band gathered there too and, after having saluted the Union Jack, we marched into school to their tunes. In the classroom before lessons commenced each morning, we stood to sing 'God Save the King', who was at that time George V. The marching ritual was repeated after lunch and each recess.

The great event of the year was the annual school concert, always held at the Mt Barker Institute in November. The choir was most important, and practice began weeks beforehand. We enjoyed folk dancing on the stage where we could all be seen, but I think we derived most pleasure from the practices. Of course, we were looking forward to the Christmas holidays which followed, when there would be a break from the long hot walks to and from school in the summer heat. The walks were not always pleasant in wet weather either but we enjoyed meeting other children along the way.

In 1923, we moved house so that Echunga School was only about three kilometres if we took short cuts, while Mt Barker was nearer six.

So we attended Echunga for about six months in 1924. There were approximately sixty children, grades I, II and III in a sort of lean-to joining the main room, where Mr Paech had the other four classes. Miss Flora Warland, a local lass, was the junior teacher.

Mr Paech introduced more outdoor activities such as caring for the school garden. One visitor was keen that we should learn about gardening. He thought that flowers could be grown for sale, especially white flowers for wreaths. He also endeavoured to stress the importance of some varieties of birds and how they helped to keep plants and trees healthy by eating the aphids and scale insects which could make trees sick or even kill them. A very interesting exercise was a demonstration on how to 'bud' and graft fruit trees.

In hindsight, I think that Mother may have disapproved of this enterprising agricultural approach in favour of a more conventional education, as we returned promptly to the Mt Barker school.

During the year, the district schools were visited by an inspector from Adelaide. We were all warned to be on good behaviour. Some of our workbooks were spread on our desks and Mr Harry would walk around casually, asking a few questions before he moved to another classroom. He drove a splendid little bay trotting horse in a hooded buggy. I felt quite honoured when he gave me a ride part of the way home one afternoon.

We rarely had other visitors but one I remember was an expert in arithmetic, elementary algebra and geometry. He impressed on us the importance of learning our tables thoroughly, so making even the longest multiplication or division simple and correct. If one remembered that $7+2=9$, $6+8=14$ and so on, there should be no problems whatever totting up those great addition exercises we were often given. Of course it was wise to check downwards as well as up, we found out for ourselves.

Miss Hilda Schmarka, who was left-handed, took us for grades V and VI. She was a splendid teacher. There were of course several changes of teachers in the various classes but the headmaster, Mr James (Jimmy)

Pryor, who managed the grade VIIs was at Mt Barker before 1920 and for some time after 1926 when I completed primary school. Eighteen of the original twenty-two obtained our Qualifying Certificate, five of us earning over 600 marks out of a possible 700.

Train Kids

The daily train from Adelaide to Victor Harbour picked up children from Ambleside, Balhannah and Mt Barker Junction for both primary and high schools. They were put off at Mt Barker railway station each morning and collected on the return trip to Adelaide in the afternoon. The Adelaide to Victor Harbour line branched at Mt Barker Junction, one track going south to Victor and the other south-east to Murray Bridge and Melbourne.

Always referred to as the 'Train Kids' by the rest of the school, they would miss the first and last lesson each day, but were expected to do some home study. Mt Barker Junction was the place to do homework and no doubt get up to pranks, although I never heard of any misadventure.

If we who had long walks to school saw them coming, we realised that we were really late and would have to explain why!

On one occasion, rather than face the train kids' teasing, Gordon and I nicked off for the day. We spent it wandering about the hills behind the Rest Home, a large and impressive building with extensive grounds – lovely for roaming in.

No children had watches in those days, so we had to guess when to eat our lunch, collect bread, papers and mail and get home somewhere about the correct time.

All would have gone well if we had not met Mrs Breandler in the paper shop. She naturally reported the unusual time that we were shopping to Mother the next time she met her. Then we did have some awkward explaining to do.

We had had a very enjoyable day but never repeated that exercise!

Bread

Beside the kitchen stove there was a large mound covered with woollen cloths and an old coat draped over the top. It was Mother's bread dough, lovingly mixed and kneaded the previous evening and left to rise overnight.

Kath Bishop and I had just washed the breakfast dishes and she dried the tray which lived on the mantelshelf above the stove. In order to replace the tray, she needed to stand on something. She was a plump child and, yes, she stood on 'the mound', with deflating results!

We looked at each other and at that moment Mother arrived screaming, 'Who stood on my bread?'

I don't know where Kath went, but I got the shaking of my life as she demanded, 'Why did you let Kath stand on the bread?'

Actually I don't remember if the bread was any worse for the treatment.

Recently Kath told me, 'I was so scared I wet my pants.'

The silly thing about the bread incident was that in a few minutes Mother herself would have knocked and punched the dough to knead it before shaping it into loaves.

School Lunches

In later years, we bought bread during lunch hour and carried it home from school, often under our arm. I wonder that it was possible to cut sandwiches from bread so treated. We always had two rounds plus a jam pasty. The pasties were made on Sunday morning; a daub of jam and a lot of pastry, rolled so that the jam could not escape. Monday they were good, Tuesday OK, Wednesday drying out, Thursday drier and Friday very dry. We ate them to the very last crumb; nobody ever wasted good food.

I had a fondness for chutney, so when a jar was opened that was what I spread for my lunch. Of course we were supposed to eat our lunch before we left the school grounds.

To walk right down to the post office for mail besides getting bread, maybe groceries, cotton or other necessity plus the daily paper, then get back to school before the first bell was really stretching things too far for me. Once, however, when Muriel Pope suddenly jolted my elbow as we crossed the bridge on our way to the street, my wicker basket with all its lovely chutney sandwiches ended in a very muddy puddle.

On odd occasions, we bought our school dinner with four pence. Two pennies bought a hot pasty or a cold saveloy (a seasoned pork sausage, in red skin). One penny bought a yeast bun, an iced finger bun, a rolled spicy London bun or maybe a Scotch cake. This latter was a concoction of spiced fruit and probably yesterday's leftover cake, a sort of plum pudding mixture between pastry crusts, iced and cut into squares. Banbury tarts, made from currants and pastry with cinnamon and sugar cost one penny.

How we gazed into the baker's shop window with mouths watering, while we made the grand decision of how to spend our precious four pennies.

By Steam Train

Under the pines near the railway station, the horse was unharnessed, tied up and given a nosebag of chaff to munch whilst Dad and I spent the day going to Adelaide to see my Gran Metcalf and some of my aunts. Dad bought tickets from the office before entering the station, where the train pulled up with a squeal of brakes and a rush of steam.

Along the platform we walked, found a carriage entrance and then a dark leather seat next to the window. We were ready for the porter's big voice, 'All Aboard!' A sharp whistle, a flag waved to the engine driver, 'choo-choo-choo' and slowly we moved forward. Then more quickly, and faster went the 'choo-choos', past the houses and on towards the hills. There was comfort in the sound of steam trains as we watched the trees and farms go by. Gradually, the steeper hills slowed the steam puffs, until, at the top of the hill with a sudden fierce burst of steam and quick 'choo-choo-choos', the train gathered speed for the descent.

'Don't put your head out the window, might get a cinder in your eye!' someone would warn, or 'We're coming to a tunnel! Close the window.'

Suddenly dark except for a dim carriage light along the ceiling then light again as we came out the other side.

It was all exciting and always we looked forward to train travel. As we left the hills, suburban Adelaide sprawled about us. There were many blocks of vacant land for it was not closely settled as we now know it. The train gave a final 'chuff' as it pulled up in the railway station, doors opened and people streamed off towards the gates.

There were electric trams in the city streets but the traffic was almost entirely horse-drawn trolleys and carts, buggies, gigs and cabs (small hire vehicles with an enclosed cab, driven from the rear). Cars were very few and caused interest for that reason. The horses tended to eye them with suspicion; some would snort or even rear onto their hind legs if the odd car backfired.

Milk, bread and meat were delivered daily in box-like carts with doors which opened at the back. The baker would transfer a few loaves into a large wicker basket and hurry to the back door, but when the butcher stopped, the housewives would go out to select their meat from the cart.

Dad left me with my Aunt Amy Dow while he attended to private business in the city, returning later to collect me for the train journey back to Mt Barker. My only memory of that visit was when Ross, Aunt Amy's son, lifted the lid off his toybox, a very startled rat leapt out!

Later, the Education Department organised a combined schools trip to Brighton or Glenelg Beach once a year. Children all agog with excitement and anticipation were collected from schools along the track.

We were first, then Littlehampton, Mt Barker Junction, Balhannah and Ambleside. Some parents accompanied us but our teachers kept a kindly eye on their charges. Picnic lunches under the jetty, family groups scattered about on the beach, it was all foreign to most country children. For many, it was their first glimpse of the sea, their first feel of fresh crisp sand under their feet, and first chilly excitement of the water.

Of course, getting everyone rounded up for the return trip was all part of the fun. Back in the train, everybody was full of chatter until mums and dads met them at the stations and gathered their tired and often sunburnt offspring home for an evening meal and a good rest. It was an event to be talked about too, the next week at school – or maybe longer…

It seems incredible now that travel is so quick and simple in a car or even by bus.

The Forgotten Jacket

Home at last!

'Hilda, Where's your coat?'

'I – er – left it at school.'

'Then go back at once and get it.'

It was no use protesting, so I started at a fair pace. I couldn't keep that up, so trudged most of the way, retrieved my coat and set off home again for the lonely three miles.

The sun had set and darkness was falling as I neared Neagle's turn-off.

Someone was coming along on a bike… Oh! My dear Dad had come to get me.

I sat on the bar and the next couple of miles seemed no distance at all.

The Institute Hall

There was a special singer visiting Mt Barker to take part in a concert and Mother, accompanied by friends, was to attend, taking me with her.

The Institute to me was a huge building with seating on either side of a long aisle. As I remember, the chairs were single with woven cane and reasonably comfortable. We sat about three rows from the front and the hall soon filled. I was to sit on Mother's knee, which made me nervous as I had often heard her say, 'Hilda is not a cuddly child.' I in turn did not think of her as a 'snuggly' person.

All went well for a while until I began to shift my legs.

'Sit still!' Mother said in a stage whisper.

Of course the more I tried to keep still, the more I would wish to move an arm or a leg, knowing I should get a slap and a 'Can't you keep still?' every time.

The people on the stage seemed to speak or sing in a most unusual manner. Oh, I was so relieved when it was all over and we could go outside into the fresh air!

Next day, we had a visitor who also had attended the concert. She and Mother were praising the acting and the singing in particular, while I was thinking, 'No one asked me what I thought.' I thought that the whole thing was silly and I could not understand a word that was said.

When I practised with other children for school concerts or plays, we enjoyed being in the Institute with its dressing rooms behind the stage and we had fun.

In our Girl Guide days, Captain Wise had us speaking from the stage so that she could hear us from the entrance door. That was quite a challenge, but it taught us to 'throw' our voices, just as the bullock drivers did when moving their teams.

By this time, there was a large Honour Roll on the wall for World War I soldiers. We could read the names and remember some of those men.

School fetes were held there too. Chairs were placed around the wall or stacked behind the stage to make room for the various stalls. Cake, produce, handiwork and of course the fruit stall for strawberries and cream. Ice cream was a real treat for one penny a cone and strawberries sixpence a serve.

When I returned to Mt Barker, it seemed to me that our large Institute hall had shrunk! I was amazed at how small it was in comparison to the size I remembered.

Circus

Dad wrapped a rug around my knees one evening as we sat in the gig (a light, two-wheeled sprung cart) to drive Prince into Mt Barker to attend a circus. I had never seen anything as big as that circus tent. It was brightly lit, possibly with gas. There were people crowding onto the long benches arranged in tiers around the ring. We found our seats and, with the crowd, watched.

The lumbering elephant – so big, picked up people with his trunk and put them onto his back. The lithe, supple clowns leapt on and then off the elephant, turned somersaults, ran, rolled along the ground, led animals, and apparently got in the way. There were trapezes and swings with girls swinging from one to another or being caught in mid-air by a chap, they would swing together and catch another swing. What really had Dad and me laughing was the funny man with baggy trousers and huge boots which turned up at the toes. He wore a bowler hat and waddled around like the well known actor Charlie Chaplin.

It had been a happy evening and I snuggled up against my father as we trotted home in the gig.

Oakbank

Easter Monday was the Oakbank Picnic Race Meeting which we attended twice. On the first occasion, I was possibly five years old. I felt very important wearing a Japanese silk frock trimmed with fine lace. Everyone seemed to be wearing fine clothes. People were picnicking in groups on the grass, with horses and buggies everywhere.

On the second visit, I was more aware of the grandeur. A little winding creek ran along the edge of the park, with small wattle and briars on its banks. As we walked towards the racetrack, we passed a small stone ford (a shallow, solid-based crossing over a creek or river), which was probably used to take the horses across. Large trees grew on the open slopes where people were chatting and picnicking. Everywhere were buggies, gigs and now some cars.

We had a wonderful day.

Just as people were packing up to go home, a frightened horse broke loose and galloped through the crowd of picnic parties causing pandemonium. Food and folk scattered in various directions. There were some injuries.

On the way home, we passed other horses and vehicles which had collided. More injuries; but bad as they were, they seem insignificant now when compared with car and other accidents caused by excessive speed, carelessness and drunkenness. Worst are the maimed, left to suffer for the rest of their lives.

At that time, we gazed in awe and admiration at motor cars as we clopped along in our horse-drawn buggy. There was always time to observe the roadsides, sheep and cattle grazing or resting in the shade as the sun reached its zenith. I was promised a baby lamb – if it was still lying by the stump on our way home. Naturally, the lamb had moved before our return.

Itinerant Travellers

Two hills rise where the Macclesfield Road runs through a gully beside a tiny creek winding its way to the main Mt Barker creek. On each hillside was a house with a white wooden gate at the entrance. Old 'Puppa' and Mrs Grimes lived on the western slope and we lived on the easterly. Swaggies often called for water or food.

One chap wanting a meal was asked to cut wood while 'the wife' prepared something for him to eat.

'You don't need any wood cut!' he said.

Dad replied, 'Well, you don't need anything to eat then.'

He left.

*

There were odd pedlars too, like Mr Moore from Griffiths Brothers, Tea Merchants.

'Here comes "More-tea",' the neighbours would say.

*

Hans was a runaway German sailor who arrived at our home early one morning – he said '…because the wind was blowing in your gateway'.

He stayed about a week doing odd jobs away from the road but he was always waiting to scan the shipping news when we children arrived home from school with the daily paper each afternoon. We had been sworn to absolute secrecy about his presence.

Many months later, a letter arrived from Hans thanking us for our hospitality. He explained that he had been caught and had spent some time in prison but was now back in Germany.

*

Bob Edgar is still an enigma to me. He lived with us for several months doing his share of jobs. He liked salt on his porridge and sour milk or cream! Bob told wonderful stories. He talked of the Greek heroes and could speak French. He even put a penny, a real shiny penny, in the hem of my frock once. A penny was a prize; threepence was a fortune in those days. With a penny, you could buy a bullseye sucker, two ha'penny sticks or almost anything! Bob always seemed special. Some years later, he called back to see us saying that his real name was Jim Edwards. I wonder what his true story was and why he left his native Scotland.

*

I liked the scissor grinders who came in a little covered horse-drawn cart in which I presumed they lived. They never pulled up at the gate but always under the shade of a sheoak tree along the roadside and walked across the paddock to collect and return our scissors. Mother obtained a still-used recipe for buttermilk cake from Mrs Scissor-Grinder.

Grimes

Old Puppa Grimes and his dear wife lived opposite. How I enjoyed the apples that she dried every year. She sat under the trees in their shade, peeled and cut her apples, dropped them into salted water, drained and spread them on trays. Every morning, the trays were placed on the roof of the enclosed lean-to back of the house and taken down each evening until the apples were just the right dryness to keep and to eat, thank you…

The Grimes had two married daughters, Gertie and Alice. Gertie and her husband, George Rogers, had three children: Vera, Myra and later George. George was still quite young when his father died of TB, the scourge of those times. As a widow, Gertie kept house for Davidsons and lived at her parents' home with her children.

Alice, Mrs Bevean, had one daughter, Rita, I suppose about my age. But Vera and Myra were much better company as far as I was concerned. They also attended Mt Barker School after their father's death.

Auntie Maud

Any holidays with Auntie Maud and Uncle Hartley Bishop were special. Uncle worked in the shop of Colten, Palmer & Preston's hardware merchants of Curry Street, Adelaide. He was round and tubby, just a little pompous but usually jolly. He had a magical wand which he used to make his smartly silk-dressed wooden doll dance on her special board while his wife played tunes on the piano.

Auntie Maud was taller and said that she was glad when Hartley had put on weight because then there did not seem to be so much difference in their sizes.

She talked of a wonderful invention called a 'to-an-frommy'. It seemed Fred Fuss, her sister's husband, had made a sort of cellar under the house to keep food cool in summer. The food was placed in a container which was put into a cupboard in the wall and lowered beneath the floor. Worked on a rope and pulley system, it was like a 'dumb waiter'. When required, it was hauled up again, and lo and behold the milk was sweet and butter firm! So necessary in the days before household refrigeration.

The only niece I ever knew her to reprimand was Brenda Bishop, who seemed to have inherited some haughty ways and gave Auntie cheek one day. That, Maud would not take.

Auntie would straighten her hair and pat some powder on her nose and remark, 'There, now I look damn near beautiful.' Her beauty was that of the inner person – the soul – and we all adored her.

I spent several lovely holidays with her, Uncle Hartley and their black and white Pomeranian dog, Tosh. Una often joined us in Byron Street, Glenelg. The Fuss family lived within walking distance of Uncle and Auntie, on or near Brighton Road.

Maud took us to the beach at Glenelg. She also took me to visit our dentist at his home in Henley Beach. He came to Mt Barker each Tuesday. To get to Henley Beach meant taking the tram into Adelaide then catching another out again. We seemed to travel miles of rattling viaducts across the reed beds before we reached our destination and then all the way back to Glenelg. Now, the reed beds are gone. West Lakes has been developed and Military Road runs from Henley to Glenelg and on to Brighton.

Maud and I set out one day to see the Duke and Duchess of York. They were to become King George VI and Queen Elizabeth (later the Queen Mother). It was a grand occasion. They were welcomed to Adelaide by a display of hundreds of schoolchildren marching, clapping, dancing and singing. From our position on the hill, we could see their Royal Highnesses in their open car as they were taken around the oval. Cheers swelled from the crowd as they passed.

My other memory of that day was that my bladder made urgent calls and no way could we reach or even see a toilet.

'Just let it go,' Auntie Maud said simply. I did, but was certainly glad to get home to a bath and a clean set of underwear.

We think Maud loved us all so much because of her own loss. Their son had died when only fifteen months old. Within a week, both his small cousin, Tommy Fuss, and their mutual grandmother had also died. The cause was believed to be food poisoning. Fermented fig jam was blamed but in summer days of the late 1890s in Broken Hill, it could have been any contaminated food.

Auntie Maud had several other pregnancies but they were not carried through. I suspect there was an Rh factor problem.

Our collections of L. M. Montgomery's *Anne* books were birthday and Christmas presents from her.

How sad we all were to see this lovely lady develop paralysis agitans (Parkinson's) and slowly fade away. I remember her saying, 'I never thought of myself as getting old, but when I was about to get on a tram today a mother held her son back and said, "Let the elderly lady get on first, John."'

She was my step-aunt, but no other aunt was just like her. I trust I showed her some gratitude for her endless kindnesses to me, and to Uncle Hartley, who always made me welcome.

Bill Paech

We often met old Bill Paech taking the cows down the hill and across the ford to their dry paddock. When his youngest son married, I think Bill met the first woman to stand up for her own rights against him, for he frequently referred to her as 'That Voman'!

In earlier days when rain was pouring, it was usual to see old Mrs Paech or the girls out in the thatched shed milking the cows, while Bill and the boys chatted comfortably in the veranda's shelter.

The New Chediston

After Granny Hunt's death in 1920, the home in which we lived had to be sold. The rest of Dad's family, being older, had all settled on their own properties.

Rowland had the original Hunt cottage at Windmill Hill with old fruit trees growing around it. A pear tree was still standing there last time I passed the property.

Harry Hunt was on 'Silvermine Hill', Uncle Sam lived in Adelaide and Uncle Pat owned Hillford Farm. Of the girls, Ethel Harrop lived between Berri and Barmera and Alice Woodland lived at Bugle Ranges.

Aunt Alice drove a smart little pony in a Masher dray (a two-wheeled cart). Her daughter Nella was older than I and later there was a son James.

Dad found a little thirty-one-acre block about three miles from Echunga. There was a long triangle of scrub, a scattering of picnantha wattles on land that had once been cultivated and some lovely old red gums. Then one reached the house, or ruins, where three plum trees stood. One was a delicious greengage.

There was a little creek which flowed after heavy rain and of course during winter. The banks were covered in blackberries. Later, we kept milking goats and tethered the billygoat on the blackberries to control their growth.

The property was called 'Chediston' because that was where my stepmother's people, the Bishops, had come from in England.

The remnants of the house had fourteen- to fifteen-inch-thick mud and straw walls, roughcast on the outside and smooth inside. The story was that the occupant, forty years previously, had been asked to leave.

Before doing so, he set alight to the cottage's thatch roof in a fit of pique. In the meantime, rabbits had burrowed under the west wall, so when Dad tried to work on that, it collapsed. However, he rebuilt it, put a new roof and later a lean-to on the northern side for a kitchen and Gordon's room.

The centre room was very cosy and we had beautiful glowing fires in the old fire place. The two bedrooms on either side had wooden floors but the living room floor was tamped earth covered with linoleum and topped with coconut or coir matting. The walls were papered and Mother did work hard to make things nice under difficult circumstances.

Dad built a bathroom, or rather general storage room with a tin bath in one corner. What was not kept in that room was not worth mentioning! Later, there were changes to the general arrangement of the rooms. Dad did try to enlarge the northern side of the house but was prevented from finishing by poor health and, like everyone else in the 1929–30 depression, had no money.

I remember odd incidents like the day I poked a pimple of tar with a matchstick in it on the side of the water tank. Dad had put it there as a temporary stopper for a leak in the tank. Of course, water spurted out and bunging it up a second time was not easy.

In summer, water was always a precious commodity despite two rainwater tanks. Every drop used for bathing, washing and so on was put into buckets and carried out to Mother's flower beds, the vegie garden or the fruit trees which they planted.

Quite a large area was enclosed for the garden, so we kept ourselves in vegetables most of the time. At the bottom north-east corner by the little creek was an old beautifully bricked well, twenty-eight feet deep. Dad cleaned it out and put a windlass on to draw up the water. Later, he erected a Dutch windmill. Dutch was the name of the local tankmaker.

When the windmill was up, with Uncle Hartley's help, he was able to install piping to the main vegetable garden. Wonderful. Until we had a frost and all the pipes burst! The mill still worked but so did we, watering with buckets carried from the tank at the mill.

However, we did grow splendid vegetables. Potatoes were planted in the back valley, maize grew well and a few sunflower plants were huge! Mother was naturally very proud of her flower garden too. In fact, it was good country for growing crops and pastures like rye grass and especially subterranean clover. Wheat grown in the Mt Barker area won first prize at a world wide trade fair in Paris about 1870.

Mt Barker's smaller agricultural areas made it unpopular for that purpose when greater tracts of land could be used in the northern areas of the state or the Murray Mallee when that was cleared.

In about 1924 or 1925, Dad purchased two blocks of adjoining land, which were hilly and partially cleared. On them he built sheds conveniently a little way uphill from our house. He also built sties for our breeding sows and boar.

There were cows to be milked morning and evening. Of course, that was a 'before school' job for me. The milk was separated, skim milk used for home cooking, feeding calves and leftovers for the pigs.

Naturally there were hens and ducks; turkeys too, were bred to sell for Christmas or Easter. I disliked intensely those young turkey gobblers. All poultry had to be penned at night, as foxes were prevalent. Foxes are very fond of any available bird. It was often my job to round the birds up in the evening. When one eventually got the turkeys together, they would stop every few yards, agitatedly making their gobble-gobble-gobbling noise. I threw sticks at them but I guess that only made them worse. It was always with relief that I shut the turkey yard door when at last I had them safely inside.

Dad had a forge for shoeing horses and other iron-working jobs, and a horse works which was used for cutting grass hay into chaff. The horse works is a capstan-like device which drives pulleys by means of bevelled gears and shafts. It was pulled by a horse walking in a circle.

The stove fire was kept burning all day, so it was necessary to always have wood on hand, gum for keeping a fire 'in' (burning slowly) or wattle for quick heat. I used to gather 'mornings wood' or 'kindling' (twigs for lighting the stove) from the scrub land. It was full of birds in the spring and summer: thrushes, bronze-wing pigeons, honeyeaters and cuckoos.

I found even more interesting the native plants. There were rock ferns springing from ledges dripping in the winter, but very dry in summer. I learned where to find orchids: blue cockatoos, spiders, monkshoods, minute mosquito and gnat orchids. Perfect they were and only one to two or three inches high (2.5–7.5 centimetres). I became very fond of this area and especially enjoyed finding plants freshly in bloom or maybe a new bird or even its nest. I could have wept when I saw a house now standing where I had once found these treasures growing freely.

My father was a good tradesman. However, when the depression came, he could no longer rely on building work to boost his income and pay the interest on the scrub blocks. Like many other people at that time, he was obliged to sell out.

Hilda Florence Metcalf, circa 1911.   *Hilda, 1917.*

Gawler Street, Mt Barker.

May Fidock, née Hunt.

Bart Hunt, circa 1917.

Uncle Hartley, Bert Bishop, Hilda, Bart Hunt, circa 1918.

Kath Bishop and Hilda, blackberry picking, circa 1918.

Harry Jessop, Gordon Dunstall and Bart Hunt, wattle barking, 1920.

Chediston, 1920s.

Gig, Mt Barker, 1920s.

Chediston shed and haystack, 1920s.

Aunt Gert and Little Gran Metcalf.

Swansea, 26th of Jan. 192[?]

Perhaps you will be surprised to hear fr.. me. But I keep my promise and let you know of my whereabouts. After I left you, I got employment at the Murray Bridge Hotel, Murray Bridge, Propr. Mr. G. I. Leaitz. I worked there till the 22nd of May, when I was found out. Well, I got 6 months H.L. but got out again after 4 days, because I was no criminal, as they thought first. The very same day I got a job on board of the norwegian sailing-vessel "Clyde" and we left Semaphore on the 21st of June bound for Falmouth (England) to await further Orders. We managed to pull into Falmouth after a passage of 142 days with the loss of three men, they were washed overboard by an overcoming sea. We had a lot of damage on deck and in the rigging. After 8 days in Falmouth, we received orders and proceeded to Swansea (Wales), here we arrived on the 25th of November. And I am still on board. We are waiting for a cargo. But I am not sure whether I will go home to Germany next week, or not. We have a very good treatment on board here and no matters of complaints whatever. That is the reason I don't like to leave the ship, and still, I should

Hans's letter, 1922.

...e. Well, how is my old ...n? — How are yourself and your wife? — and Gordon & Hilda? — Have you still got Prince & Dolly? — And old Bob? — Well, Mr. Hunt, I may thank you and your wife again very, very much for the treatment I received by you, and for keeping me there. And I am sure that when I happen to be in Adelaide or Melbourne, I will run up to Mount Barker and pay you a visit. But in the proper way, I would not run away again from a ship, it is too much trouble. You may write to my home address in Germany and they will send the letter after me. But before that, I'd always let you know of my whereabouts. Hoping that I will have an answer from you

I remain,

with my best regards and wishes
to you and your wife,

Your most sincere
Hans Möller.
ex Wood-chopper.

Best regards to Gordon and Hilda.

Write please to this address:
Hans Möller
c/o Leonh. Krey
Rathausstr. 8 III
Germany   Hamburg 1.

Marian Hunt, separating milk and cream, 1923.

Ford, 18033, Mt Barker, circa 1924–25.

Auntie Maud with Trixie, Glenelg.

Thelma Fidock, milking, circa 1925.

Hilda aged 12, May 1925.

Horses, Mt Barker, circa 1926.

Uncle Pat Hunt's tobacco crop, circa 1926.

Coolgardie safe.

Hilda and Donald Farmer, Chediston, circa 1927.

Hilda on Darby, Chediston, 1929.

Betty Bell, Hilda Hunt, Mavis Colebatch, 1929.

Hilda's report card, 1929.

Marian and Bart Hunt, Chediston, 1932.

Hilda aged 21, 1933.

Marian, 1937.

Tommy Hunt

Dad was a small quiet man, his name Bartley Thomas Hunt. His family called him 'Tom', his cronies referred to him as 'Tommy 'Unt' and Mother always called him 'Bart'.

Apart from farm work, he was a builder, bricklayer and carpenter; trades learned from his Cornish/Welsh father and his brother, Harry. At times, he would undertake building jobs away from home. This meant camping during the week, coming home only for the weekend and fresh food supplies.

Occasionally, Mother and I, and once her brother Perce, would harness the horse into the buggy and visit Dad on the job. Probably we would be taking him some extra rations. These trips were always of interest, new places to see, different roads from our usual trips to Mt Barker. It was more interesting than whizzing along in a car. One could see the sheep and lambs, the cattle, horses, birds, crops and farmers working. Uncle Perce pointed out a hawk hovering above some mouse or cricket and made counting magpies into a game.

I guess Dad would never have become a union man, as he was not only a stonemason and bricklayer but would put the roof on the house as well. Of course, money was never plentiful, so any work apart from the few milking cows, wood or wattlebark, helped his income.

He was rather fond of wine and would sometimes come home from a sale a little the worse for that. But he always saw that his horses were well fed and watered. Those horses seemed to enjoy being groomed, talked to and fondled by a gentle hand. Of course, they had to pull hard too in boggy creeks or when ploughing land for potatoes, oats or other crops.

Dad made pigsties from split logs with a sloping half roof thatched with tussock straw or even boughs. What squealing, smelly animals pigs seemed to be when shut in such confined spaces. One morning, one of the farrowing sows was missing, so naturally Dad had to look for her. When he had tracked her down, he came back to the house, to take me over to the rising ground she had chosen to have her babies. There under a huge pile of tussocks, heaving and grunting contentedly was our black sow, with her thirteen little piglets drinking and suckling. How she must have worked, digging out tussocks with her snout and carrying them to the area she had chosen to farrow in. It was certainly cleaner than any sty. She had made her bed so well that we could see neither her nor her piglets until she was disturbed. It took the rest of the day to drive her and her family back to her pen. It really seemed a shame to do so when she had gone to so much trouble, but Dad was extremely patient in guiding her back – with everyone else's help of course. She reared her thirteen piglets, runt and all!

Often on Sale Day, Tuesday, after the pigs and calves and so on had gone under the hammer, there would be a few boxes of 'sundries' to be sold. These could hold nuts, bolts, saucepans or other odd equipment which Tommy 'Unt picked up for a 'bob' (one shilling or twenty cents) or two. We found it fascinating to poke into these, to find a pencil, a ruler or tape measure, nails, a picture frame, enamel mugs – anything almost! One saucepan just held two rabbits for pot roasting. They made a delicious meal.

He enjoyed hunting rabbits because they are such destructive little animals and a rabbit was a welcome addition to our diet. Very occasionally he shot a pigeon and once even some parrots. When Uncle Perce or Hartley came to stay, they enjoyed going out too, and once they visited an area near Caloote to shoot ducks. Somehow with all the packing and checking of camping gear, guns and food, they left the ammunition home. They of course could not return for it in a horse-drawn vehicle, so they contented themselves by catching yabbies. Oh! What a wonderful feed of yabbies we had that Easter Monday!

Afterwards, the saying went, 'A lot of galoots went to Caloote.'

That was the night we discovered that we had an invasion of rats. The shells from the yabbies had been put into a large pan to be taken to the chooks next morning but when Mother went into the kitchen, the dish had been emptied and remnants of yabby shells and claws were scattered all over the floor or dragged towards a hole behind the skirting board. Then followed an anti-rat campaign. The two dogs were most enthusiastic, poking under floors and into sheds and dark places. Many rats were caught but the invaders were never completely eradicated.

Odds and Ends

On the fertile hillside and in the little gully, *Chou moellier* and mangelwurzels were grown to feed the milking cows.

Chou moellier, of the cabbage family, grew large leaves up a metre tall stem. As they were pulled off for cow fodder, the stalks grew taller producing more leaves for summer feed.

Mangelwurzels were a type of beet with large leaves which were gathered for the cattle. Later, the huge beets were also chopped for stock feed.

Potatoes were cultivated for marketing and household use. We grew 'carmens', 'snowflakes' and 'up-to-dates'. Some folk spoke of 'pink-eyes'. As seed potatoes grown in one area were said to 'run out', fresh seed from Mt Gambier was brought in as new stock.

*

All children were taught to milk cows and feed the calves at an early age. One learned to dodge the sharp lashes from the cow's switching tail and the firm stamp of her foot on our own, or worse still, her foot in the bucket! The top of Dad's hat was an excellent receptacle for a little drink of fresh milk, still warm, for Biddy, the spoilt white Pomeranian dog.

Many things happened to cows. One fell down an old well and had to be hauled out in a most undignified manner. Poor old Darkie, another of our milking cows, found the supply of bran and pollard for fowls' food. Unfortunately for her, she knocked a box of nails into the bran. They punctured her paunch and she died of bloat.

Often, they jumped fences to wander miles in search of a bull. Of course, someone had to walk an equal number of miles to find the cow and bring her back for milking.

∧

As we walked to school daily, any offers for a ride were gratefully accepted. Tuesday was Bennett and Fisher's sale day. Carts loaded with pigs, trolleys with calves or cows, and buggies with people rumbled past. Choices were fairly wide, but sometimes there was no room for us.

A pig escaping from a spring cart caused its owner quite a chase near Breandler's farm on one occasion. I think we were late for school being entertained by the antics of both pig and owner!

Rides were more frequent on the way home with empty carts and trolleys.

*

Dad always enjoyed watching a good 'wrastling' match.

Market Day

Every Tuesday at Mt Barker; gigs, buggies, drays and wagons converged on the town and especially to the sale yards at the lower end of Gawler Street. It was Market Day!

Because Jacobs Smallgoods manufacturing company in Mt Barker managed the bacon factory, pigs were the main line. Usually in addition were calves, some cattle, sheep – not many – a horse or two maybe, and finishing up with boxes of sundries, containing anything from nuts, bolts and old lamps to stoves.

Donahue's blacksmith shop was conveniently located next-door to the saleyards. What a great atmosphere! The smell of burning charcoal, hot iron, the acrid odour of burnt horn as the hot shoe was applied to the hoof and the ring of the blacksmith's hammer on the anvil. Of course, every farmer had his own forge, hammers, tongs and anvil at home for the small jobs which were forever cropping up.

The visiting dentist rented a room in the pub next to the yards and we children went there for treatment.

I remember being intrigued by the chatter of the German farmers when they met in the street. I could not understand a word of course for they spoke in German, even though the practice had been frowned upon during the 1914–18 war. They spoke in English when conversing with us. We thought them strange then, but now I realise they had the advantage over us because they had two languages. I don't remember any child of German extraction speaking anything other than English at school or elsewhere.

Sale day was my Uncle Pat's particular day. He was employed by Bennett & Fisher's, the local stock agent, to help with yarding and marking of stock. He donned blue denim pants and shirt and with his pots of green or yellow paint, daubed the squealing pigs and bawling calves as they were yarded and later brought up to be sold. Needless to say, Uncle Pat's clothes were well smeared in green and yellow by the end of the day.

The Chinese gardeners, Lee Sue's from the Piccadilly area, always had a well patronised fruit and vegetable stall in Mt Barker's main street on Tuesdays.

No Seamstress

After Aunt Ethel's death, the knitting lay around until I was about ten, when Mother suggested that I knit Dad some socks.

I had no problem following Ethel's written instructions for turning the heel and decreasing for the toe. I know not how long it took me to knit a pair of socks but I remember that it seemed easy. I suppose it was one thing I could do that Mother could not. I even started to crochet and made a doll's jumper in four-ply grey wool with purple trimming.

Now, sewing was a different kettle of fish. The girls at school could always make even running stiches and hems. Lucy Paltridge's satin stitches were satiny smooth and neat. Mine in contrast were wildly uneven – cat's teeth, I think they called them!

Darning in theory is simple. Over and under, over and under, but mine seemed to get two over or two under or 'sumfthun'. One day, I thought, 'I'm really going to get this right.' And I did. No missed threads. I was so proud of Dad's darned sock that I took it to show Mother. So much for pride.

'You've done it on the wrong side' was her only remark.

My deflation was prompt and at the great age of eight or nine I decided it was absolutely hopeless to try to do things perfectly for Mother.

Now I often wonder how often I deflated the ego of my own children. I also know that many children who never get any praise are, in some perverse way, naughty just to gain attention, even though it may be punishment or scolding.

Crocheting is great and quick, and the infinite variety of stitch effects, are, to say the least, fascinating. But I can knit without watching my work – while watching TV or when riding in the car – although reading is my favourite accompaniment. Later during my married life on a rural property where distances were a factor, I utilised travelling time by knitting for my husband and children.

My ambitions never ran to millions of dollars but surely I have exceeded the million in knitted stitches!

Show Days

The Mt Barker Agricultural Show was held early in March. A lovely autumn show with mature vegetables, beautiful fresh fruits and watermelon…only a penny for a large slice, lush pink flesh spotted with shiny black seeds to spit out and deep green rind. It still makes my mouth water. How the juice oozed and was likely to be dribbled down one's best clothes, usually a white voile frock with lace insertion, white socks and black patent leather shoes. A wide-brimmed straw hat with an elastic chin strap was sometimes daringly trimmed with coloured flowers.

Everyone went to the show. All one's school chums could meet and wander together. We peered at the common and strange types of poultry, cattle, sheep, particularly the fat Romneys of Edgar Davidson's. We watched the horses with their riders trotting, cantering and jumping, in the ring events. Not to be missed was the Grand Parade with smartly harnessed horses in buggies and gigs brightly painted or varnished to a fine sheen. Beautiful carthorses were a lighter build than the hefty Clydesdales.

Motor cars were still reasonably rare but becoming more popular, along with one-ton trucks and the Bluebird charabanc (a flat-topped vehicle with rows of bench seats for large excursions) which did not belong to the show but took passengers from Adelaide to Strathalbyn via Mylor and Echunga. It was a sort of bus. Bert Pope and his son, Cliff, eventually bought the Bluebird, cut its body down and turned it into a truck. They used it to carry twenty-gallon carbide tins in which to gather food refuse from hotels and boarding houses for pig slops. Oh, how sour was the smell.

One show day we stayed at home barking wattle trees. It was a beautiful day too and we could hear the traffic along the Macclesfield road heading for the show. No doubt I was envying the watermelon eaters.

Old Jack Ross

On the eastern side of the Macclesfield Road opposite his field pea paddock, Ben Paech owned another eighty-acre block of land. A little creek wound along the centre of it and filled a small waterhole before flowing on to join the Mt Barker creek. Near the waterhole was a corrugated-iron hut in which an elderly man known as Old Jack Ross lived. He was quiet person who we sometimes saw walking to or from Mt Barker for his supplies, mail or pension.

Perhaps he was shy. I do not ever remember him speaking to anyone. Some years later, while perusing old newspapers, I came across an obituary notice of a Mr John Ross who had been one of the men working with Charles Todd when they built the telegraph line from Adelaide to Darwin. Suddenly I realised that this was our Jack Ross who lived such a lonely life. Although we had been taught about this event at school, we were unaware that we had in our midst a person who had taken part in Australian history. When I mentioned it to Cousin May, she said that he was known as a quiet man who lived with his books.

Incidentally, Phil Yeatman's father was the Adelaide postal telegraph official who received the first message that was sent from Darwin to Adelaide on that line. Una Farmer, my step-cousin, later married Phil Yeatman.

Galahs

Wherever we travel, flocks of galahs, with their raucous erratic flight, are the most common birds, particularly during early morning or near sundown.

As a child in the Adelaide hills, the only galahs or other cockatoos we saw were caged birds or chained to a perch calling 'Pretty Cocky', 'Cocky wants a drink' or 'Hello, Cocky'. They were great mimics, kept for companionship and because they were rare.

The first galahs we ever saw in the south-east were two birds near Argyle on our way to Millicent. Jack and I stopped the car to show them to our two children, Ian and Jean, in 1946 or maybe 1947. How these birds have increased in numbers in the intervening years.

We know that the white man and his activities have been the cause of the great build-up of populations of cockatoos and corellas as well as galahs. Waterholes, windmills and bores have provided permanent drinking water, farming and cropping of the land means huge areas of freshly sown wheat or shooting grain can provide acres to forage on, allowing the birds to breed into pest numbers. They strip young leaves from eucalypts along creeks and watercourses in our northern areas. The trees look as did those in Western Australia after a cyclone had gone through the area, but a cyclone is only an occasional disaster. The birds return to their trees ripping off any fresh green shoots and will eventually cause the trees to die or at best sprout odd side-shoots. But it's illegal to shoot the birds. The laws of common sense never seem to apply!

Curlew

It was Dad who called me outside one evening at dusk to listen to a curlew. From some distance up the gully, I could hear a long drawn-out eerie call which seemed to echo down to us. They must have been becoming rare in the hills at that time, for I never remember hearing that sound again. Jack said the last time he heard a curlew call was when working at Wattle Range in the 1940s. We heard a similar cry on the lakes in Canada, which was the call of the loon. They were on the far side of the lake and had one young or maybe two with them.

Once when driving along the Onkaparinga River road to gather blackberries, Dad stopped the horse and buggy and took us back to see a goanna which, when we startled it, had run a metre or two up a large gum tree and was clinging to the trunk.

I had had bronchitis and on my first day outside afterwards, Dad brought me a bunch of bright pinkish-red flowers which he called ladies' fingers. Many times later, I was able to gather them myself, and many other native flowers as well. I learnt the particular places in which some of these plants preferred to grow. Ladies' fingers I now know to be *Grevillea Lavendulacea*. These never seemed to grow more than twelve to fifteen inches high (30–45 centimetres) in those areas.

Here and There on Western Flat

'Cook-cack, cook-ack' the wattlebirds call in the blue gums still. They called like that when I wandered along the dirt track to see my Aunt Mime.

I did love meandering through the scrub from my earliest times until I left home. The whole area was more or less still scrub with patches cleared along the gullies for potatoes, crops or gardens. Sometimes the topsoil was removed to expose the red ironstone gravel – buckshot – which was used to seal the roads.

Kath Bishop and I were poking about in the scrub one day looking into hollow logs and things. Hidden in a hole in a tree we found a square tin box. I recognised it as my father's, so we carried it home. On the way, it was accidentally dropped. The lid came off and out fell sawdust and several detonators. Unconcernedly, we replaced them and delivered the box to Mother, who was horrified!

Detonators were used to blast out dried tree stumps when clearing land. Land clearing was heavy slogging, cutting and grubbing of trees and undergrowth. Consequently, the stumps of larger trees can still be seen in some older paddocks.

Aunt Mime and Uncle Harry lived on a small farm called 'Silvermine Hill'. The four-roomed mud-brick cottage had a small lean-to kitchen from whence came delicious aromas. Aunty Mime always found some particular treat for me when I came. Maybe passionfruit and cream or freshly baked Johnny cakes which we took up the three huge ironstone steps to eat in the dining room.

Because of our early relationship, Aunt Mime remained special to me all her life.

They had an orchard of mixed young fruit trees, including a cherry, which to my recollection was unusual. Apples were in plenty, plums, quinces and pears, peaches and nectarines too, but not cherry trees.

When Charlie left high school, he kept bees, rows of hives in the sheltered gully a little distance from the house which always seemed to smell of honey and honeycomb in the summer.

Dad kept bees too, but only an odd hive or so, or he would rob a swarm from a tree he knew of. One extremely hot New Year's Day, he elected to rob his hives. He set up the extractor to put the frames in after they had been decapped using a hot knife frequently dipped in a bucket of hot water on the stove. All was progressing well, honey, honeycomb, someone turning the handle of the extractor, bowls to catch the honey, an odd bee or two buzzing and everything generally hot and sticky.

Down the long hill came a motor car – a load of visitors to see my Dad. To say that Mother was not amused would put it mildly! They were a nice friendly family bringing New Year wishes. Of course, people just dropped in – telephones were few and far between. I guess Mother was embarrassed at having been caught in such a sticky mess.

Friends and Neighbours

One of our closest neighbours, Mr Halliwell and his family, lived in a sheltered gully off the Echunga road. The house looked cosily nestled at the foot of a drive, which left the road from the top of a steep hill. Maybe some of the windows did have glass but the ones I saw had unbleached calico tacked to the frames.

Bees were his life interest. He had planted a double row of sugar gums (*eucalyptus cladocalyx*) along the driveway when he went to live there 'farty years ago'. A little old man in a dark suit, Mr Halliwell always wore a veil over his hat while tending the bees.

Once, he had owned a horse and cart but had been tipped out. It must have really upset him, for he never trusted another horse and always walked to town. His daughter rode a bike even though the track up Halliwell's Hill was a quagmire in winter and always deeply rutted.

After his wife died, old age forced him to go to live with his married daughter near the Mt Barker showgrounds. He took some of his beloved bees with him, much to the consternation of the locals.

Symonds acquired the property then and developed a quarry for road metal from a hill further back from the road. They put a new home on the hillside close to the road. Dad built the concrete house, which went up in twelve-inch layers. The outside was roughcast with crushed metal and cement. Dad also had the job of realigning the road on Halliwell's Hill and gravelling it so that we could drive up. Now it is a sealed road.

Actually, Gordon and I became, in time, rather fond of that portion of Echunga Road from where it turned off the Macclesfield road. On the left, what had been Beckie Abbott's became McDonalds, adjoining our own little thirty-one-acre block. On the right was Bill Paech's. The first paddock frequently held the dairy shorthorn bull. We gave him a wide berth. He wore a bull baffler, which probably did not improve his temper. This contraption was a shield over the eyes; it tipped forward for the animal to feed but covered his eyes when his head was lifted.

Then there were Paech's sheds and house with pine trees surrounding them. Further down the hill their garden, always so well tended, grew vegetables and plenty of onions for the family and huge mangel-wurzels and *chou moellier* for cattle fodder in summer. The garden was hidden from the road by a wide but magnificent briar hedge. Dressed in springtime pink and green, it smelt delicious. In autumn, the leaves turned golden and the briar berries glowed brick red. They contrasted the darker red of the high hawthorn hedge on McDonald's side of the slope down to the foot bridge and paved ford. How the Adelaide rosellas loved those hedges!

Across the creek, we turned off and cut across McDonald's paddock, thus missing Halliwell's Hill and shortening our trip by half a mile or so.

*

Mrs Thompson was a dear chatty old soul who dropped her aitches with abandon, to my delight. Eggs selling for sixpence a dozen caused her to remark, 'Hain't heggs cheap, Mrs 'unt?'

When she said that they were going to visit Harrogate, I was at a loss to know whether or not Harrogate really did begin with an aitch.

*

Having to take a message to Mrs Breandlar on my way to school once, I asked if Olga was ready to leave.

In her high penetrating voice, she replied, 'Olga! She's gone already yet!'

Hillford Farm

The only way we ever went to Uncle Pat's was to walk. From the house of my grandmother, the path went up a little creek with briar bushes near tiny pools, past the waterhole with the huge blackwood tree, where the horses and cows could drink, until it came to the swamp where I had once heard the curlew call. Here was the fence and a back road. Any unmade road between two properties was a back road. Now they are 'made' roads and often sealed. Across this road was the gate into Uncle Pat's land, where he later planted his little apple orchard.

It was not far to the house with its huge spreading mulberry tree on the western corner. How we enjoyed those mulberries. The house was large and rather rambling. Along the north-east side, a long large room was used as a kitchen and general living room.

One tragic day, Madge Baker committed suicide in front of the huge fireplace. She was a teenager who helped Aunt Em with the children. Cousins of Uncle Pat and my Dad, Madge and her brother were orphans who had been brought up by Aunt Em's parents, the Fidocks. She used a pitchfork to press against the trigger of a shotgun… I was never told the whole story, but one can imagine the impact of a shotgun blast to a girl's head.

Eventually, the big room was demolished and two new rooms built. We enjoyed visiting at odd times and on special occasions such as Christmas when a large tree was decorated. I don't remember much tinsel, but there were candles and blown egg shells hanging in coloured woollen 'cradles'. They also acquired an Edison gramophone with its large horn-like trumpet and dozens of cylinder type records which we loved to play and listen to.

Mollie was just younger than I, John a year younger again and Douglas came about three years after that. He was a bit of a horror but I always thought that his father egged him on.

Near the house, partly sunk into the hillside, was a cellar. One stepped down inside the door between wide stone benches where milk pans, before the days of separators, stood for the cream to rise. Next day, the cream was skimmed off with a slightly curved, perforated tin disc, about eight inches in diameter. It was put in a bowl to make into butter for the family and for sale in the local grocer's shop. Skimmed milk was fed to calves or pigs. Later, separated cream was put into cans and taken to the Mt Barker railway station, to be delivered to Balhannah, where Spoehrs had a butter factory.

Cleanliness was essential in these dairies, for the smell of soured milk became quite offensive and persistent, and attracted flies. We had not even heard of refrigeration. The Coolgardie Safe (a wooden-framed box covered by wet hessian, keeping contents cooler by evaporation) was one compromise to hot weather. Often, articles were let down a well on a rope, the well being the coolest place on most farms. Butter was also placed under a wet cloth.

Milk separators were quicker and more hygienic than the many milk pans and skimmers. The milk was fed by gravity from a large container bowl into a spinning cylinder. The lighter cream separated from the milk, both of which flowed from different spouts into a bowl for the cream and buckets for the milk. The cylinder was spun by a series of wheels and cogs driven by the operator (often me) turning the handle at a steady sixty revolutions per minute. As soon as the operation was over, the whole contraption was dismantled, rinsed in cold water, washed in hot water, rinsed again and drained ready for the next episode.

On top of this dairy was a little attic room which one entered from a door at the opposite end or back of the building. We children found it a lovely sheltered hideaway to play or read a book or comic.

Sinks and draining boards were unknown in the kitchen and when

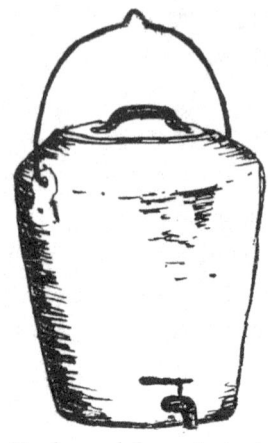

they were introduced were wooden and not stainless steel as we know them today. A meal over, dishes were stacked on a table; out came the wash-up dish and a large tray to drain the dishes on. Water, of course, was kept hot on the stove in heavy kettles or the iron fountain with its long shining brass spout and tap.

Washing up over, tea towels were hung to dry by the stove, the dish stored away and table cleared. But it did not finish there. Kettles and fountain had to be refilled with rainwater from the tank outside. Many an iron kettle has been ruined by boiling it dry.

Beyond the house were large sheds, stables and pigsties. Pigs were reared and fattened to sell at the weekly Tuesday market, where Uncle Pat worked. A big fair man, Uncle Pat was pleasant and easy-going, but he once put a whip around Gordon's shoulders because Gordon had pointed a toy gun at him.

At the opposite end of the yard was a row of low, tangled fig trees, the delight of Aunt Em's chooks and shelter for odd pigs when they escaped from their pen or sty.

Past the fig trees was the 'dub' or lavatory. Melva George once came flying out of it yelling, 'Aunt Em! There's a hen under the seat with a nest full of ripe eggs!'

I never heard whether the eggs were really 'ripe', or if mother hen brought out a clutch of multicoloured chickens.

Aunt Em had a loud voice and did not hesitate to say what she thought, but we all knew where we stood. I never knew her to fly into fits of rage like Mother.

When We Were Younger

Maybe I was scared stiff of my stepmother with her sudden outbursts of violent temper and bitter biting tongue, but living with her also had advantages to a timid country child. She had friends and relatives living in Adelaide suburbs where I spent many happy hours and pleasant holidays.

The first I can recall was staying with Mother's niece Kath Bishop. Kath had an older sister Brenda and a brother Bert, rather a wag. It was he who taught us to play donkey drivers. With plug tobacco tins for carts and bent treacle tin lids for donkeys, we made teams of six, eight or ten donkeys, two abreast to haul the carts. Into the folds of the lids we punched two holes front and back. Through these holes, thin wire was threaded and bent into 'c' hooks for hitching the 'donkeys' and carts together.

We gathered ironstone to build fences and yards in which to paddock our donkeys. Ironstones, the common stone of the area, were only three or four inches in diameter and easy to handle. The whole ménage was kept in a carefully cleared patch of ground some distance from the house.

The children's widowed mother, Auntie Myrtle Bishop, was a tailoress and thus eked out a meagre income. Her husband, Perce Bishop, had died in October 1918 of TB; as did his sister Ethel in 1919. Dad often took loads of firewood to the Bishops.

Bert Bishop had learnt about donkeys and camels when his father was sent to Farina, south of Marree, to be in a drier climate for his health. I doubt if the family lived there for a year. It was too late to help his condition.

Kath and I had some lollies one day when we needed to visit the toilet, generally known as the WC (double-u-see) or 'dub' for short and always situated in the backyard. Kath announced that 'to eat in the dub was to feed the devil'! In other words, it was unclean to eat there. An early lesson in hygiene!

We two girls were playing in the backyard when we heard the tinkle of a bell. Kath recognised this as the call of the Ice Cream Man. She rushed inside to get a penny for each of us from her mother. We both ran out to the street and there was the man with his small horse-drawn box cart driving along ringing his bell for the children to come and buy. A whole ice cream for one penny! We felt rich indeed as we licked our ice cream while the man with his bell, cart and ice cream went on down the street. Other children rushed out to him with their pennies just as we had.

Once when at the Bishops, I had no white frock, the correct attire at that time to wear to Sunday school. Auntie Myrt found one of Rhona's, another niece. It had been worn, but appeared clean, so I wore the white voile frock. During the lesson, my nose bled, as it often did. Alas for the white dress. Mother was quite put out that I should have soiled it.

Kath often came to Mt Barker too. Years later, I went to visit her in her own home and wondered if we would recognise each other. As I walked to her house, I heard her voice. Of course I would know her by that if nothing else!

Another place where I often stayed was next to the Croydon railway station. The Leaver family lived there with their six adult children. The youngest boy, red-headed Reg, brought me a chocolate, to eat in my bed at seven o'clock in the morning, just to welcome me. Their mother, who I called Auntie Di, had been a schoolfriend of my stepmother's.

Auntie would suggest that it would be nice to have a yeast cake for morning lunch and give me a shilling to go to the baker's shop for it.

In the sitting room on the mantelshelf sat a beautiful brass camel. I picked it up to examine more closely, little suspecting that the saddle was really the lid of an inkwell. Oh! My brown and white check frock…

But Auntie Di only said, 'How lucky that I'm doing the washing. Take it off and pop it right into the tub.'

The dress came out perfectly free from ink. How I loved this kind friendly woman.

My own Aunt Gert Metcalf lived nearby and Little Gran was staying with her at that time, so I could visit them also.

I think the place I most often stayed was with the Farmers at 44 George Street, Clarence Park. Russell was a big boy when I first remember him; the twins, Muriel and Flo, were eight years older than I, Jean elevenish, Una a little younger than I. John was a small boy and later there was delicate Donald, who died from rheumatic fever. Uncle Horace was a saw doctor and worked, I think, at A. Pengelly and Co., where the trams were made for Adelaide transport.* Auntie Myrt was naturally kept busy with her large family but always made me feel welcome.

Una and I spent many hours playing in the backyard. Sometimes we walked to Plympton to see the Bishops, but our special delight was to visit Uncle Hartley and Auntie Maud at Glenelg. We nieces were her children and she knew just how little and bigger girls liked to be treated.

We went on errands and took messages for Una's mother. One elderly friend was a Mrs Slate, who told us she had once known a Mrs Bran and a Mrs Pollard but they did not mix! Bran and pollard were traditionally mixed together for poultry food.

On holidays to Mt Barker, Una loved it when my dad let us get out and walk or scamper along the roadside while the horses laboured slowly up the hills – hard to imagine with today's motor traffic.

We two girls spent many happy hours together. We learned to cro-

---

* A. Pengelly and Co., of South Road, Edwardstown, built tram bodies, railway carriages, furniture and, later, motor cars.

chet by making dolls' clothes. I also rather envied Una's agility. Why, she could turn cartwheels and many other contortions. I was not even allowed to try to turn somersaults. Why? Because someone might see my pants? Oh, how life has changed and viewpoints too.

I saw my granddaughter, Tess, gracefully turning cartwheels in the yard. At once I was seven or eight years old again. It was a beautiful summer evening. The world felt grand. Gordon began somersaulting among the stooks of oaten hay, Indian tepees standing in lines along the side of the little hill near the house. I joined him. Oh, the wonderful feeling as I rolled over, clumsily no doubt, as I was considered an awkward child.

Suddenly I was brought to a halt. Mother's voice, 'Hilda! What do you think you're doing? Get up at once! Such behaviour! Why, I could see your pants!'

I had learned long ago not to argue. Getting to my feet, I felt dirty, unclean, humiliated. What had I done? As far as I knew, my pants were clean. Gordon could roll about as much as he liked, but little girls, no! No! No!

Macclesfield Road

At the foot of the hill were some lovely old pear trees and the original dwelling, probably of slabs and thatched with bark or hay, had stood nearby. There had been a well for water supply, long since covered and forgotten. However, wandering stock must have dislodged the cover and a cow fell in. Of course, it somehow had to be hauled out, so Dad got his brother Pat to help him.

They tied ropes around the cow and hitched them onto a harnessed horse and oh, what pulling and shouting and pushing went on, until eventually a very wet, dirty and sore cow was safely landed onto firm ground! Weary men and horse were relieved and needed refreshment. The well was then filled in completely.

Poisoned Hand

One morning, Dad complained to Mother that his hand was sore. She looked at it and scoffed, 'If you had some of my problems, you'd have something to complain about.'

Poor Dad went off to the shed nursing his hand. When he could bear it no longer, he returned to the house with his hand badly swollen, looking like a ham of meat.

Mother immediately showed her concern and, as Dr Auricht from Hahndorf was visiting Echunga that day, she harnessed the horse and took Dad there. The doctor made many incisions along the hand and ordered saline baths but it did not improve. Although Dad spent several days in the Adelaide Hospital, when he returned home he had lost the forefinger joint of his right hand. It would have been very awkward but he seemed to cope and work as hard as ever.

Water

So many towns now have reticulated water systems that we tend to forget that water is a very precious gift. We expect it to flow by turning on a tap in our well fitted bathrooms. Washing machines and dishwashers use water freely and irrigated gardens thrive. We are told that lawns are our most expensive non-profit crop.

The story in the 1880s was a very different one, those folk fortunate enough to have iron roofs on their homes carefully directed rain into tanks or more often dug an underground tank, sealing the sides with cement plaster. The water was drawn up in buckets or a windlass was erected. Later, Douglas pumps saved much hard work.

In the south-east of the state, channels were dug to drain water away. Even so, a shallow bore found water.

Where I grew up, rain rushed down the hillsides into little creeks and on to larger ones. At times, there were only disconnected pools which dried as summer approached. It was necessary to enlarge the pools and catchment areas to form waterholes or dams. Many folk depended on wells for a water supply. After being dug, the sides were shored up with logs, stones or bricks. Superbly constructed, they lasted for years. Again came the slow process of drawing water. Full to almost overflowing in winter, the levels of both wells and dams sank and even dried up as summer dragged into autumn. Rainwater tanks were essential.

In 1890 in Broken Hill, the water was carted from the Menindee Lakes by bullock teams. It was supplied to residents in hundred-gallon square tanks for seven shillings and sixpence (75 cents per 450 litres). An ounce packet of Epsom salts (28.35 grams) was added to settle the ever present red dust.

In the cities, water was reticulated to houses but elsewhere every drop had to be carried in buckets to be heated in the copper or inside for household use, and filling of kettles and fountain. At the edge of the stove stood the fountain, a large container with a tap at the front to supply at least three gallons (about fourteen litres) of hot water. No wonder people bathed only weekly. The whole family often used the same water, which was then carefully carried outside to nurture some precious plants or vegetables.

Mother used to tell of their family's bath in the late 1870s. She, Hartley, Ethel and Syd had a bath on Saturday afternoon, were dressed in clean clothes, given half an apple and allowed to go walking along the beach at Port Lincoln.

In the 1920s, it was not so very different. Each morning during the week, we washed our necks, ears, faces, hands, knees and, I suppose, 'possible'. Saturday was bath night. Water was heated in a kerosene tin on the stove. In winter, a tub was placed in front of the kitchen fire and the serious business of getting clean began. This little horror dreaded the ordeal, which usually ended in tears and a slap, until my step-cousin Flo Farmer gave me a bath when I was almost seven years old.

Eventually, a tin bath arrived, which was put in the corner of an outside room. Besides being draughty, the room held all manner of things, old coats for example and preserving jars. The tin tub had an outlet hole but the water was usually tipped out. Outside the back door stood a wooden bench with a hand bowl for washing hands and face before meals.

I once remember being stunned because my Aunt Mime's neck was very dirty. Perhaps it was Friday or Saturday and she was due for her bath.

Water for stock sometimes became scarce and it was often my job to take the milking cows to the ford road crossing, over a mile distant. It was a usually pleasant trek. On one occasion, Mother's niece, Kath Bishop, was with me. Halfway down Halliwell's Hill, I found a frill-necked lizard on a post. Quickly grabbing his tail, I took him to the water too. While at the ford, he escaped to the nearest deep pool, inflated himself and floated in the centre. With a stick and by holding onto an overhanging branch, I managed to recover him and returned him to his original fence post. Naturally, he had more than enough of Kath and me; he leapt off the post and scampered away into Paech's dry grassy paddock.

Washing Day

The night before, kindling wood had to be gathered for the copper. To fill the copper and the triple set of troughs, all water naturally had to be carried from the rainwater tank in winter and spring, or from the well when rainwater was getting low. The copper was filled, kindling set for quick lighting the next day and longer sticks piled ready to stoke up the fire as necessary. No one seemed to have taps over troughs, or bath for that matter. We were fortunate to have troughs, as many people still used the old iron tubs. When the washing was finished, again the water was bucketed away. In summer, it was carefully given to special plants or shrubs, which in the hill country became very dry. Recycling!

We used four-gallon (18-litre) kerosene buckets for all liquid carrying purposes, except for milk from the cows. Kerosene was used for all lamps and lanterns, and was always procured in square tins, two to a wooden case. The cases also had many uses for storage or stacked as shelves. Sometimes, the sides were removed from the tins which were then returned to the case and used as drawers as we had in our cabin cum kitchen and later spare room at 'Kintyre'.

I have digressed… Mother never had a regular washing day, which meant that when clean sheets and clothes ran out, she had a really big job ahead. One of my Saturday jobs was to wash and iron my school blouses and underwear.

While the fire was heating the copper, yellow soap was sliced, chipped or grated. When the hot water had been transferred to the troughs, the soap was put into two to three inches (six to seven centimetres) of hot water and boiled to dissolve it before adding more water and the clothes.

The soap? Burfords No. 1 in a bar, cut into five or six blocks for convenience, was generally used. Sometimes, Mother made her own soap with fat rendered from suet, caustic soda, resin, borax and water. (In the 1940s, we sold tallow fat for seven shillings and sixpence (75 cents) per kerosene tin. Later it became unsellable.)

There were of course other brands of household soaps in the grocery shops. One brand was Preservene. An advertisement for this was displayed in the city tramcars. A woman's head and pointed finger nodded to and fro as the tram rattled along its tracks. The caption read, 'Washing Day, 7.30 and nothing dirty.' It did not state at which time she began her washing!

The clothes were all sorted, dirty patches soaked, cuffs and collars or knees of pants well soaped after being spread on the scrubbing board for this purpose. The copper fire was stoked up again and sheets and other white articles boiled for twenty minutes. Sometimes, borax was used to soften hard water when rainwater became low in late summer. All whites had a final rinse in water coloured slightly with Reckitt's Blue to keep them looking white.

Tablecloths, cotton frocks and other items were dipped in thin starch solution, which meant that when dry they had to be sprinkled with water and rolled ready for ironing. The detachable collars on men's shirts were always starched. Luckily, Dad didn't wear many special shirts.

When the whites were hung out, there was always the assortment of coloured clothes, heavy men's work trousers and lastly socks.

Everything except sheets and tea towels had to be ironed, using flat irons heated on the wood stove, rubbed clean of smoke or smut by wiping over beeswax covered with a rough cloth.

No wonder Mother disliked washing day!

Dad always said, 'It's safer to keep away from the house when washing is in progress!'

Of course, ironing was rarely done on the same day as the wash. I'm sure Mother would have been delighted with some of the modern drip-dry materials. Tea towels were not ironed as she said they dried better when rough dry. As for washing machines, I fear they would never have done the job as thoroughly as she did. She was always conscientious.

A Glimpse of Beauty

In a chain of little pools which were always left in the creek bed when the spate had subsided, was a tiny pool, shaded by a briar bush with its red fruits. There at the edge to drink had come a beautiful bronze-wing pigeon. Quite unaware of my watching, he began to bathe and preen his feathers. What a peaceful and beautiful sight. I slipped away so as not to disturb such tranquillity.

Maybe I was ten or twelve years old, I do not know, but the scene remained as a pleasure to be recalled. Many such moments occur throughout life to smooth away some of the harsher scenes.

Tannery

Acacia Picnantha – how gloriously golden were the blossoms in springtime, but autumn was the season when the bark stripped most easily. Wattle barking was an annual job.

As a small child, I often enjoyed spending the day with my Dad when he was out in the paddocks. I remember him cutting sapling wattles where they had grown thickly, straight and tall, probably after the area had been burned. The saplings were one to two centimetres thick and maybe up to two metres high. Dad cut them close to the ground and gathered them into bundles, leaves and all. The bundles were stacked on a trolley drawn by two horses and taken to the tannery in town to be crushed while still green.

More often, however, the larger trees were stripped. A slash was made in the trunk about seventy centimetres from the ground and bent over. First he stripped the stump and then the rest of the tree as far as the branches and leaves. The stripped bark was laid out flat to dry and later tied in bundles for convenience of loading, delivery and weighing. Our hands became tough, rough and brown-stained from tannin in the bark.

Stripped wattle wood burned well and Mother always used it for a quick fire for boiling kettles or baking scones. Wattle wood with the bark dried on never burned as well as the stripped wood. The trash from the twigs and leaves was burnt in the autumn and winter rains would ensure a good regrowth of wattle seedlings which took six or seven years to mature. If trash was burnt in the spring, there was no regrowth but a dry dusty patch waiting for thistles and other weeds.

Autumn is the correct time for rehabilitation of the Australian bush.

I enjoyed trips to the weighbridge at the tannery by the smelly tan-stained delivery ramp. The iron tyres of the trolleys and the shod hooves of the horses crushed the dropped and broken pieces into an acrid brown mush along the driveway. On wet days at the delivery area, bark squelched underfoot and the smell of tannin, the works, drying skins and hides was everywhere. One always associated this distinctive odour with the tannery.

Local farmers and butchers delivered skins and hides from all slaughtered animals. Fresh skins were freely sprinkled with coarse salt and rolled up to be delivered at the earliest convenience.

We heard on radio and TV in July 1982 that the Mt Barker tannery had closed down. It had stood for a hundred years and over a hundred employees became redundant. Now I hear a supermart has been built there.

To my knowledge, it had always been managed by members of the Paltridge family. In Gawler Street, Paltridges also had a boot and shoe store which one entered by ascending several steps. The floor of the store was the ceiling of an underground room where bootmakers cut, tacked and stitched sturdy boots and shoes for the local community. The workroom had windows at street level, through which we children could watch the cobblers plying their craft. I doubt if the light admitted via these ground level windows was very efficient in wintertime.

Our boots were lace-ups, coming well above the ankles and strong

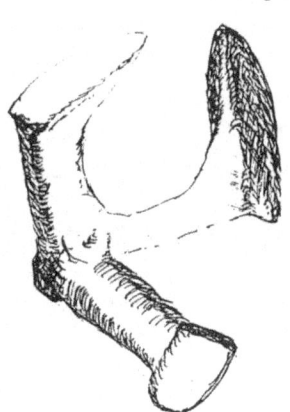

for walking on country roads; wet weather or fine. Occasionally, a tack would protrude inside our boots, but we could hammer down any offending points on Dad's last. A last is a three-legged contraption with one leg finished to fit into the heel of a boot and the other two, one large and one smaller, to fit inside the upper.

Our first duty, after having something to eat when we arrived home from school, was to change our clothes and clean our boots with blackening and of course shine them ready for next morning.

Of course, wattles also grew, along roadsides. These trees were stripped by workmen who needed employment. It also ensured that the wattles did not become old and die before being replaced by new growth, thus keeping roadsides reasonably fresh and tidy.

No one can deny the beauty of a golden wattle tree in full bloom.

Autumn

Autumn was always an enjoyable season. There were blackberries to gather, fruit and vegetables to harvest, Easter and the Agricultural Show. You could buy penny slices of watermelon, large and dripping juice from its lush, seed-spotted pink flesh.

Autumn colours glowed on all the European trees and hedges, so lovingly cultivated by our English and German forebears. We children scuffed our way along the school paths with leaves scrunching.

People still spoke of going 'home' to England, even though they and sometimes their parents had been born in Australia. It is no wonder, therefore, that they grew English trees and had English gardens. Australia's beautiful native plants were only scrub to be cleared and burnt so that crops could be planted and stock fed.

Lights

The old gaslights were replaced by electricity in the early 1920s. Oh, the magic wonder of being able to get a light by the flick of a switch. Naturally, that was for town use only. Later, some farms had wind lights or engines but most of us continued to use kerosene lamps and lanterns. The lamp glasses could get smoked so washing and polishing these glass chimneys was a regular duty.

Wood

Wood collecting and carrying from the wood heap was a daily chore and not grumbled about, for without it we would have had no wood for warmth or for cooking. The lighted stove was a welcome sight and everyone enjoyed the glow from an open fire on a chilly evening. The logs varied from gum or stringy bark (eucalypt) to sheoak (casuarina). Some of it was axe split for the stove or for getting the fire going.

It became my task at weekends to collect enough tea tree sticks or light wood for the following week. Actually, I enjoyed poking around in the tea tree finding flowers, orchids, watching birds or even making up my own stories.

Easter Time

Easter was fun. Often, visitors came to stay: the Perce Bishop family, Uncle Hartley with our adored Auntie Maud, and another time Auntie Di Leaver. There was usually some special place to visit, which meant early rising, horses to be fed, groomed and harnessed plus preparing of chaff with bran for later. Of course, there was a great basket spread for ourselves with preparations made over previous days. Pies and pasties were baked and poultry killed, dressed and cooked. Food was carefully stored away from ever present blowflies. and the Coolgardie safe used to keep the butter from melting in warmer weather.

Uncle Perce took me mushrooming in Becky Abbott's sheep country once. The creek which ran right through the property was most often a series of little waterholes containing yabbies, grey 'muddies' and little silvery spotted 'butterfish' – delicious fried. But first we gathered the worms, threaded the hook and waited all agog hoping for a bite

'Wow! I've got one! No, he's gone.'

'Never mind, try again.'

And again and again… Once, we did get more than a dozen.

Blackberry time: a day for a picnic along the Onkaparinga River near Mylor, between two government experimental farms. As far as I can recall, the experiments must have been to do with fruit orchard production, for there were many fruit trees, including golden medlars near the fence. However, our business was to do with picking the blackberries that hung in clusters from the bramble-covered banks.

Standing in cool trickling shallow water rewarded us with the most lush and juicy fruit. Smudges on our faces told that not all the berries went into our tins! We ate our fill of the sweet ripe fruit and gathered them in small buckets which were emptied into kerosene tin buckets. The adults picked busily until everyone decided it was lunchtime. Back to the buggy, where the horse stood unharnessed but tied to the fence munching chaff from a nosebag.

Mother always excelled herself with picnic lunches on such occasions, which were enjoyable and relaxed. A rug was spread out with a tablecloth on top and everyone sat around the edge. Plates were filled with poultry, lettuce, tomatoes and followed by apple pie or cakes. Table manners were eased for once.

Berry picking was resumed until late in the afternoon. Tired, scratched and grubby, we packed everything away, including kerosene tins filled with fruit. The horse was rested and ready to head off. Everyone crowded into the buggy for a happy drive home, counting magpies or recounting events. It was along this track that Dad stopped to let us look at a large goanna which had scuttled out of our way and up a tree trunk.

Visitors always brought us Easter eggs. A white sugary concoction joined by scallopy pink, blue or yellow icing and with a yellow fluffy chicken emerging from the hole on top. Nibbling the coloured icing allowed us to open the egg into two pieces and share the sweets inside. Once, I had an egg with a ship stuck to the top. I never did work out the connection between the chicken, the hen, the egg and the ship!

Uncle Hartley always saw the Easter Hen, but she had just disappeared over the sheoak tree when we arrived!

Dunny Cart

I would doubt if any 'night carts' or 'dunny carts' exist today, but in the 1920s, 1930s and even into the 1960s, where the country towns had no sewerage systems, these carts were still in use for the disposal of human waste.

Toilets were always outside the house, a little building down the yard. They had a wooden seat with a galvanised metal can underneath and usually a small trapdoor at the back where the full can could be removed and replaced by a clean can. On farms, 'night soil' was buried out in the paddocks. In towns, full cans were collected on a cart and taken to pits or scrub where the contents could be tipped or used as filling. The cans were then washed, painted with tar for hygiene purposes and replaced on the trolley ready for the next round.

The carts I knew of were sturdy trolleys drawn by two well-cared-for horses. The driver sat forward, as was usual in all trolleys. A person was contracted by local councils to carry out this duty weekly – usually in the early mornings. I guess it was an unpleasant but very necessary job before the days of flush toilets.

At one time, Uncle Harry had the job. Later, he became a councillor. At least he would have known the back entrances to every yard in the town and the condition of the streets. The horses, too, would have known when to go and when to stop.

One of our neighbours, old Mr Echert, later became 'night man' for two to three years. He had a sturdy trolley drawn by two fine light draught horses for his odorous cans. He was known for his agreement with most things, drawling, 'Thaa-at's true' after each statement. Once, he was heard to remark. 'Thaa-t's true, I finished on the cart,' doubtless with explicit adjectives too.

It was usual to have in each toilet a bucket of ashes with a small tin to scoop out ash to sprinkle over faeces to minimise odour and thus flies. Newspaper squares were often cut and hung from a nail on the wall. In our toilet, newspapers were kept whole so that one could read entire articles without being cut-off.

Colloquial names for these small buildings were numerous: Little House, Dunny, Dub, Privvy and WC among other things.

Comparisons

During the bicentennial year (1988) we older people reminisced, especially about how things were done. At a WAB meeting, each of us was asked to record some earlier experiences or those we knew of. The houses or lack of them! Joan Kemp remembered her grandfather's cheese factory at Glencoe and the two-hundred-gallon (900-litre) square tanks of whey, which local farmers used for feeding their pigs. There were washtubs, scrubbing boards and hand wringers. I mentioned the introduction of hard-hoofed animals and how their feet cut up the country or plugged up water holes. Animals went wild. We now have feral pigs, horses (brumbies), camels, foxes, rabbits and hungry cats (the damage they cause in the bush), sparrows, starlings and the rest.

There was little or nowhere for hospitalisation; a doctor was miles away and no telephone. The doctor rode his horse or drove a buggy.

Someone recently commented that bread was threepence a two-pound loaf in the 1930s. I beg to differ – four pence in early 1920s and four pence ha'penny for years. I wonder how many sandwich loaves I carried home under my arm for almost four miles on schooldays. After all that hugging, it was a wonder anyone could cut decent sandwiches next day for lunch. Mother did and later I had the job. No pre-cut bread then.

Salt was one penny a pound and sugar four pence ha'penny. Root vegetables – carrots, turnips, beetroot and so on – four pence a bunch of four roots of reasonable size. The prices never seemed to keep rising as happens now.

Unbleached calico at sixpence a yard could make many tough-wearing things and would bleach white quite soon.

Remember ha'penny confectionary sticks and the pleasure of choosing pink, yellow, red or green? Cherry Ripe was sixpence if you had sixpence. Nestlé's chocolate blocks at one penny, bigger ones threepence, sixpence and so on. Mrs Wiley with her little shop near the school had amazing patience while we chose our sticks, coloured marble lollies or jubes, when and if we had the money.

Horses

Violet of my early memories was a medium carthorse, plough horse and useful general purpose animal. Bay in colour with dark mane and tail and only one eye – I almost forgot the white blaze of her face. Dad was proud of her in a way. She could always be trusted to bring him home and, it seems, take folk to Mt Barker. Marian and Myrt harnessed Violet to go to town. By the new Catholic church, the council workmen did laugh heartily at the two townie drivers of the horse with no bit in her mouth! Violet took us to Mt Barker often, to school or shops, to catch a train, to visit family or friends. She was part of life and she knew it. We loved her despite or maybe because of her 'wall-eye'. In Violet's days, cars were seldom seen.

Clippity-clop, clippity-clop, home we go in the spring cart. Down the hill comes old Mr Watson with his horse and cart. Violet stops in her tracks and we all shoot forward.

Mr Watson shouts, 'Whoa' to his horse and pulls the reins.

We resettle ourselves on the seat and prepare for the two men to have a yarn.

Dad acquired our shiny-coated chestnut Prince as a young gelding of reputedly good breeding, but with the dropped lip and pot belly of a motherless foal. He was lighter than Violet, but was fitted into use for cart, plough, trolley and buggy quite often too. We had him for years, with others I have now forgotten. Eventually, to Mother's disgust, Dad let Uncle Pat have him. She thought that Pat would have less feeling for him than my dad.

Marian and Maud harnessed our pretty little cream-maned chestnut to the sulky to go driving. Bonny was so fresh and frisky that they only drove to the gate, turned him round and came back to the shed!

My own first pony, Topsy, was black and had been owned by one of the local butchers. At cantering, she was not the best, but how she could trot or chase a cow and loved to do so. My only fall from her was when I failed to move as quickly as she did while turning our roan cow whose calf had been sold at the market the previous day. We got the cow back home again, or I should say Topsy did. When Topsy came, I was twelve years old and in grade seven. I rode her to school, leaving her in Choat's chaff yards, where I fed and watered her. I also rode her to pick mulberries from the huge old tree growing in Choat's yard along the Mt Barker creek.

It was a pleasure for me to take her to Donahue's shoeing forge beside the sale yards whenever her shoes needed attention. I loved the atmosphere: the aromas of charcoal burning in the forge fire, blown to a bright glow by a pull on the handle of the bellows (big wooden bellows with sort of concertina sides), the acrid smell of burning hoof when the hot iron scorched it; backed by the ringing sounds of hammer, shoe and anvil. They were part of life at home too. Charcoal came from gum wood burnt in a specially made pit kiln.

I had enough mischief in me to let Muriel Pope try out Topsy when I knew that she had no idea of rising in the saddle. There was no other way of making Topsy go, except trot; and trot she did. Muriel soon gladly let me have her back.

I loved that horse. She was a companion and how I missed her when she was replaced by a bicycle. It was all very shiny and new, but needed a lot of leg power to get up or, partway up the hills. I soon learned to pick good tracks and keep out of the loose gravel on the road edges.

After the bike was sold, we obtained Darby, a sturdy little thickset pony, looking rather like the ponies of the English downs or moorlands. He had several tricks which he always tried on new riders, but once he realised who was boss, he was steady and reliable for riding or in the buggy.

When the Port Lincoln School boys were visiting Mt Barker High School, cricket was the game. Coralie Willis received a 'wang' in the eye from the cricket ball. I took her in our buggy leading her rather wild-going steed out to her home in Flaxley. Of course there was a 'Please explain where you've been until this time' when I arrived home. In those days, there were not many telephones around in country homes.

Another time, Dad and I picked up a buggy and two ponies in Adelaide. We left Clarence Park about two p.m. with one pony in the shafts and the other on a lead behind. By the time we reached the Devil's Elbow, it had started raining and it kept on steadily all the way through Stirling, Mylor and Echunga. We eventually arrived home wet, tired and cold at about ten p.m. The hot meal was appreciated when we finally explained to Mother why we had bought a buggy which did not have a hood.

The back of the buggy seat forever after showed the rubbed wearing caused by the wet rope of the lead from the horse behind. Once, we camped behind a shed at Eagle on the Hill. Dad did not consider the brakes safe for travelling through the hills, winding down to the Devil's Elbow and beyond on a dark night.

When the horses were doing the long haul from Devil's Elbow up to Eagle on the Hill, we used to get out and walk, run or play along the roadside. On a moonlight night, crisp and clear, I remember Cousin Una and I having our legs well wrapped in newspaper to keep out the frost.

Echunga Road

It must have been about 1925 when one day Dad came home with a 1914 model Ford car for £100. Not many folk at that time had a car. Dad had never driven a vehicle which was not horse-drawn, so he had to learn how to manipulate this car.

We had a gently sloping hill with wattle trees scattered about the slope, so Dad used them as obstacles. Each day after the evening meal, he would crank up the car and drive by meandering through and among the wattles. The Lizzie's lights glowed brightly when the engine revved but almost faded away each time he slowed down. Up and down, in and out went those lights for several days until Dad was satisfied with his newly acquired ability. Then he was ready to try out a trip to town and all went well.

Gordon and I would sit in the back while Mother sat stiffly in the front next to Dad. Her comments rather annoyed us.

'Oh! Do be careful, Bart!'

'Look out, Bart!'

'Mind, there's someone coming!'

Dad just kept his calm and used the controls as he thought necessary. I guess Mother never really learned to relax in any road vehicle, as years later she would grab for the side or the seat at the least sign of a turn or swerve.

Soon after our Ford arrived, Uncle Pat bought one. He asked Dad to give him a few hints and help him learn to drive. Dad walked over to his brother's place on Christmas morning, planning to be home for Christmas dinner. Dinner was all ready but there was no sign of my father coming home across McDonald's paddocks until about three o'clock in the afternoon. Uncle Pat had run into a gate post! Naturally, things had to be straightened out, although I understood that the damage was not serious.

After a year or more, Dad decided that a truck would be of much more use than the car. Dad bought a one-ton Commer truck to transport wood, wattle bark and other commodities to Mt Barker more quickly than with the horses.

Uncle Pat took our, by this time old, Prince, but I still had my pony.

Loads of firewood were taken to Adelaide for the Bishops and the Farmers in an hour instead of about four hours by horse-drawn vehicle. Dad really had cared for his horses. They were fed and groomed, and working horses were never made to trot or race as one sometimes sees on television these days. But they often had to haul heavy loads up hills and through creeks, or plough wet and heavy soils.

This had been a relatively easy time financially, but soon the depression began and times became extremely difficult, eventually causing the loss of all the property and a move to Barmera, in the Riverland.

Hammond

In October 1927, almost a year after I had left primary school, it was decided that I should spend a month up north at Hammond with my Aunt Laura, her husband Uncle Arthur Crisp and their children, Lance, Burt, Verna and Rex. Rex was about one year younger than I. He was at that time attending high school at Quorn, travelling there by train on Monday and back on Fridays.

We had arranged to meet my dear Little Gran Metcalf at the Adelaide railway station. Auntie Maud accompanied me to the station but no Gran. Evidently a mix-up! A misunderstanding. Luckily, Auntie Maud met the Metcalfs at the gate on her way hone and arranged that Gran would follow me on the next day's train. We both arrived safely.

On my first morning there, Uncle Arthur took me outside to show me the red dusty plain stretching away into the horizon. The Flinders Ranges rose dimly far off.

'You can't see that far at Mt Barker,' he said. He loved that dry land. Even though there was no crop that year, he had seen it covered with waving golden wheat. After harvest, the laden wagons would line up at the railway station to offload their grain. The family had photographs to prove it.

Arthur Crisp had taken laden horse-drawn wagons through the winding Pt Germein Gorge to load into boats anchored off the long wharf. One time when crossing Whim Creek with a team, he had been caught in a flash flood, common after a downpour in the far-off ranges. He climbed into a red gum tree, collecting wagon and horses downstream later. I never heard what condition horses or wagon were in when all gathered together again.

Despite poor prospects, the folk had a happy disposition. All were struggling with similar problems. In the hills, I knew some people who owned more than their neighbours and liked everyone else to know. Snobbery is a cruel trait of our society. Mother was a superb example, but Dad treated all his friends alike, be they rich or poor. In fact, I know he once helped a bankrupt grocer to do a moonlight flit.

Singing songs around the piano in the evening was a common activity. Burt and Verna loved singing together and were in demand for local concerts. They all played tennis at Willowie on Saturdays.

I was taken to the little Wesleyan church at Amyton for Sunday service. The heat had shrunken the timber in the ceiling so that bits of straw from troublesome sparrows' nests poked through. Our little Gran had laid the foundation stone of that church on 14 October 1878. The building has disappeared now, but I heard that Les Mills had taken charge of the foundation stone. Les was a friend of the family who later married Verna.

The sheds and stables in this area seemed to have their roofs made from boughs topped with many layers of hay thatch, which made ideal sleeping and nesting places for numerous sparrows. One of Rex's entertainments was to go to the shed after dark and bang old square kerosene tins with a stick. Out would fly the startled birds to be caught by Rex's flaying stick or by hand to have their necks wrung. I have seen growing crops mere shreds, stripped of their grain for two to three hundred metres by hungry birds.

One pleasant experience was a visit to the Melrose Agricultural Show. It was held in beautiful grounds under the shadow of Mt Remarkable. The creek is wide there; dry, like most northern waterways except when in spate. I do not know if the narrow swing bridge still crosses it, but it would sway ominously if too many folk used it at once!

Of the many splendid exhibits, I remember a really beautiful and delicately coloured aquilegia plant.

Another day we went to Booleroo Centre, crossing the creek at Booleroo Whim. A sister of Les Mills lived in the centre and while we were there, an elderly man entered the room.

My little Gran (at seventy-two) immediately rose and skipped across the floor as if she was only sixteen. 'How wonderful to see you, Bert. It's over fifty years since we last met,' she exclaimed. She and Bert Mills had grown up together and Bert was an uncle of Les Mills.

It was at Hammond that I first became really aware of a howling wind. Every three to four days, a wind seemed to come, raising the red dusty earth with it, so that the verandas were soon covered with thick layers of rippled red dust. It was so dim indoors that lamps were lit and the white globes of the old Bismarck lamps became visibly redder. So did my Little Gran's hair as she sat reading. Any article lifted from the table left a clean area of its basic shape, while outside the wind continued to whistle and whine about and around the building. Verna told me how, when coming home from school on windy days, they had to follow the fence line for about three miles (4.8 kilometres) along a three-chain-wide (60-metre) road or they would have become lost. The cattle had running eyes, which formed a muddy channel down their faces and there seemed to be almost nothing for them to eat.

When one cow calved, Verna asked, 'What are we going to feed her on?'

When it did rain, the roads became dangerously slippery!

The good seasons may have been good but they became less frequent. Eventually, Rex and his parents went to Inman Valley on the Fleurieu Peninsula (relatively fertile and green). Verna and Les stayed on at Willowie but later moved to Adelaide. Lance worked on the railways and Bert was killed when he crashed his motorbike into an unlit wagon one night in 1932.

On a later visit north, I was staying with Les and Verna at 'Heath Farm', Willowie. We were to take a picnic lunch and visit a gorge in the ranges where Les knew there were some Aboriginal drawings. We arrived at a gateway leading to the gorge when down fell a very sudden sharp shower. Les, knowing how treacherous those tracks are when wet, wondered if we should proceed further, so we waited until the rain stopped and the sun came out to shine on a glistening, wet world. A native pine (*Callitris*) standing inside the gateway turned into a spectacle of sparkling beauty. No Christmas tree I saw ever seemed as glorious as that rain-sprinkled tree kissed by sunshine. We continued into the gorge, the name of which I have unfortunately forgotten, but the beauty of one tree remains with me in memory of a lovely afternoon in our inspiring Flinders Ranges.

High School – 1929 and 1930

It was usual in the 1920s to leave school at the age of fourteen years and work either at home or seek some employment. I left at fourteen, after obtaining my qualifying certificate with a 93% pass. Muriel Stevenson topped with 95%. Her twin Norman, Lucy Paltridge and Alice Smith also did well in that 1926 year. I was at home for two years and, as work was difficult to obtain, because the depression was beginning, I started at Mt Barker High School in 1929 at Easter and spent two years there.

It was a wise decision, probably principally made by Mother, though Dad considered it good too. I feel that I have benefited all my life from that experience, I think as much or more from the teachers and their personal attention as from mixing with the other pupils. I was two years older than classmates, although some from my old class (1926), like Muriel Stevenson, Betty Bell and one or two of the boys were in the leaving class. Although I did my second year certificate, I and all our class failed dismally in maths.

I usually travelled to school by riding my podgy, shaggy but sturdy pony Darby. At times, I drove him in the buggy to get provisions or a bag of chaff for his feed when it was needed. When driving, our neighbour's eldest lad, Ross Leibelt, came with me. His horse experience was limited and I was highly amused to see Ross leap from the buggy when Darby turned sharply and threatened to tip the four-wheeler over. All Ross should have done was rein Darby into the left-hand direction instead of to the right-hand. Horse riding or driving, bicycles or walking was the usual way to travel.

A welcome addition was a shed where we could put our ponies and harness.

I found work at the high school enjoyable despite, or maybe because of, the long hours of milking cows before and after school as well as my studies.

My schooling finished for a second time at the end of 1930. In 1931, when the depression was intense, there was work at home but money was extremely scarce. The depression was affecting everyone no matter what their status. I had applied to become a nurse at the Adelaide Hospital and was waiting to be called up for training in November, when I would be nineteen.

Mother organised the clothes necessary for me, and Auntie Maud Bishop made up all my uniform frocks and aprons. I remember having a made-over frock of Mother's for street wear.

Mother certainly found times difficult. Everyone lived off the land, if possible growing one's own produce, and rabbits were a tasty meal. Mother was an excellent cook. It was such a shame that this kindly helpful woman should have such a flaring temper and bitter, biting tongue. Life with her was very difficult and complaint was absolutely out of the question. I found those months in 1931 almost intolerable, and my dad must have felt the same way.

The call came early, in September, asking me to report to the Royal Adelaide Hospital on 10 October – how wonderful.

I said quietly to my dad, 'I prayed for this.'

Just as quietly, he replied, 'So did I.'

Oh, my dear father, how quietly understanding he was. I have often wished that I had been more thoughtful and loving towards him. Although I'm sure he knew I loved him, I never said.

We had very little time together afterwards as he and Mother struggled with the failing finances of those times.

Barmera

Having to sell all their property during the depression in 1934 must have been a bitter blow to Dad and Mother. They took the few belongings they had left and set up house in a little cottage in Barmera about where the caravan park is now. Dad obtained a job in a local butcher shop in the main street, an easy walk from the cottage.

I visited them there before going to Melbourne Women's Hospital with Min Seakamp to do our midwifery training. We had completed our general training at the Royal Adelaide Hospital, Min in August and I in October. Min went to Northfield Infectious Diseases Hospital and when I finished, I joined her there while we awaited our call to Melbourne. It came in October 1935. Min by this time had completed her year at Northfield. I had to return after completing midwifery to get my Infectious Diseases Certificate, which I did the following year.

In December 1935, Mother had visited Adelaide. She brought back with her for Dad a pair of bathers. Because the weather at Barmera was so warm, she thought Dad would like to go swimming in Lake Bonney, which was just at the lower end of the property they lived on. Dad was happy to do so, but must have become too cold for that night he became ill and next day was taken to the Barmera Hospital with pneumonia. His heart, having been affected by typhoid fever in 1910, could not cope with the strain so he died on 22 December.

Matron was not keen to let me have leave, but of course did so on learning of my father's death. Uncle Russ Theobald, who lived in Melbourne, helped by lending me extra money for the train fare to Murray Bridge, where his sister met and took me to the Theobald home until the train for Barmera came. That was a great help to me as I had three or four hours to fill in. Mother and Uncle Hartley were waiting for me at Barmera where we buried my dad on 24 December, the day after my arrival and of course Christmas Eve.

The local folk were kind and helpful. Uncle Hartley had to return to Adelaide and his Maud. I stayed in Barmera four weeks. We sold Mother's furniture and she took the rest of her meagre belongings back to Adelaide.

I returned to Melbourne, leaving my dad in a lonely grave in Barmera. Last time I was there, I found his sister Ethel Harrop was buried nearby about two years later. She and her family had lived at Glossop, I presume from when she married early in the twentieth century.

It is only in later years that I have realised what a very special person my dad was. I guess we often do not appreciate the goodness in people until it is too late.

Blakiston

It was not very long before Mother acquired a cottage at Littlehampton, where she lived for three or four years. It seemed to me that this was one of the happier times of her life. She found some of her old Mt Barker friends and also joined the Church of England at Blakiston, where they were preparing for the church's centenary. I think that my grandparents Hunt were married in that church; their graves are in the churchyard cemetery, as is that of my great-grandmother Moseley. Mother never mentioned their graves but surely she would have known? Was her dislike of my grandmother so intense that she would not tell me?

Mother did enjoy helping with the centenary preparations. One of the oldest country churches in South Australia, it has a slate floor and polished pews. I've only visited it once but would like to do so again.

Postscript

On completing my midwifery training, I went to work in the southeast of South Australia, where I met Jack. We married in 1940 and settled on a farm near Hatherleigh until 1975, when we retired to Beachport.

After Mother left Blakiston, she lived in Auntie Myrtle Bishop's cottage at South Plympton in Adelaide. When she could no longer look after herself, she came to live with us on the farm at 'Kintyre'.

Although she was not bedridden, it became too difficult for me to cope with her by myself, so she returned to Adelaide and was placed in care at a nursing home. During the next fourteen years, she moved a few times to other homes. Flo Farmer tended to her personal needs.

She passed away in May 1972 in her ninety-ninth year.

www.ingramcontent.com/pod-product-compliance
Lightning Source LLC
Chambersburg PA
CBHW070916080526
44589CB00013B/1322